20942.

KT-476-279

Tel: 01962 624760

Faith or Fear?

A Reader in Pastoral Care and Counselling

WINCHESTER SCHOOL OF MISSION

05977

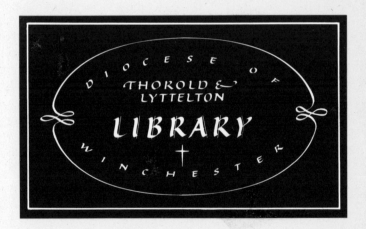

DIOCESE OF

THOROLD &
LYTTELTON

LIBRARY

WINCHESTER

RR A44

Faith or Fear?

A Reader in Pastoral Care and Counselling

EDITED BY MICHAEL JACOBS

Darton, Longman and Todd
London

First published in 1987 by
Darton, Longman and Todd Ltd
89 Lillie Road, London SW6 1UD

Introduction and arrangement © 1987 Michael Jacobs

ISBN 0 232 51718 5

British Library Cataloguing in Publication Data

Faith or fear?: a reader in pastoral care
and counselling.
1. Pastoral counselling.
I. Jacobs, Michael, *1941–*
253.5   BV4012.2

ISBN 0–232–51718–5

Phototypeset by Input Typesetting Ltd, London SW19 8DR
Printed and bound in Great Britain by
Anchor Brendon Ltd, Tiptree, Essex

Contents

Part IV: The Nature of Pastoral Ministry

Part V: Faith and Personality

Part VI: The Critique of Pastoral Counselling

Preface

Compiling a reader is rather like being asked to choose ten desert-island discs; or even like being asked at an interview what books one has read lately. The mind alternates between going blank but also not knowing where to begin, since the choice is so wide.

To assist me in what felt like a daunting task, I wrote to over forty people who teach pastoral studies and/or pastoral care and counselling. Each was asked for ten suggestions for inclusion in a reader on pastoral care and counselling. It would have been impossible to handle four hundred different choices, but fortunately others obviously felt as bemused by the task as I initially was, and the lists received were not always long; interestingly, there was very little overlap in the suggestions received, and yet I think that I have probably included something from nearly every list that was returned to me. Not that I set out to do so, because what was clear from the replies was that there were so many different fields within pastoral care and counselling, that more than one reader could have been produced. In the end I opted for my own particular interests, although drawing upon the suggestions sent to me. In reading some of the texts sent in to me by my correspondents I have learned much from the material; in the way that I hope the reader will, both from this selection and from following up the original books or articles. In the end, of course, the choice has to be mine, and I have to take full responsibility for any significant omissions; but I wish to convey my thanks to all those who sent me their ideas, for their helpful reactions to the proposal.

I am told that my own writing is quite condensed, and that I do not waste words. If in editing I have been equally rigorous, there is some hope that I have been able to highlight key passages in the authors used; but the danger is that I have assumed a continuity between passages which my search for conciseness has excised. I hope that I have not distorted any author's meaning by omitting a crucial qualifying sentence. The awareness-raised reader will be conscious of sexist language in some places – obviously much of this material comes from a period when authors were less aware than they are now of the sensitivity to these issues. I have taken out most footnotes from these readings, except where they are essential to the sense, or where they cross-refer to other texts in this reader. I have added footnotes in order to clarify the occasional technical term, and to assist with the task of cross-referencing. Obviously the person who wishes to pursue other references should go back to the original. The titles given to the extracts are in nearly every case my own, but I have preserved original sub-headings wherever possible.

The acknowledgements to authors and publishers follow this preface, but I wish also to record my thanks to Lesley Riddle of Darton, Longman and Todd for the original idea and her assistance with the technicalities of compiling a reader; and to my secretary, Mrs Barbara Hackney, for her careful work in writing for and keeping track of the enormous number of necessary permissions. The experience of a summer school with the staff and students of the East Midlands Ministerial Training Course provided me with my title, and confirmation of the importance of the selected theme; I trust that this reader will be of value to them and to all students of pastoral counselling and other pastoral studies.

MICHAEL JACOBS

Leicester, October 1986

Acknowledgements

The editor and publishers are grateful to the following for permission to use copyright material: Allen and Unwin for *Psychology for Ministers and Social Workers* by H.Guntrip; the Revd Paul Ballard (editor of *The Foundations of Pastoral Studies and Practical Theology*) and the Revd Dr Stephen Pattison, author of the article taken from that book; Basil Blackwell Publishers, for *The Psychoanalysis of Culture* by C.R.Badcock; the editor of *Contact* and the following contributors to that journal: Dr R.J.Elford, Mrs Irene Bloomfield, the late Dr James Mathers and Professor A.O.Dyson; Darton, Longman and Todd Ltd for *Rediscovering Pastoral Care* by A.V.Campbell and *Tight Corners in Pastoral Counselling* by F.Lake; Faber and Faber Ltd for permission to use *Young Man Luther* by Erik Erikson; Sigmund Freud Copyrights Ltd, the Institute of Psycho-analysis and the Hogarth Press for permission to quote from Volume IX of *The Standard Edition of the Complete Psychological Works of Sigmund Freud* translated and edited by James Strachey; Harper and Row Publishers, Inc., San Francisco, for *Stages of Faith: The Psychology of Human Development and the Quest for Meaning* by J.Fowler; the Editor of *The Journal of Pastoral Care* and the following contributors to that journal: Professor Thomas C.Oden, the Revd Dr Terry Creagh, the Revd Joan Hemenway, the Revd Dr W.E.Baldridge, the Revd J.J.Gleason, Jr, the Revd Dr. Quentin L.Hand, the Revd Professor Shirley C.Guthrie, Jr; the Kappa Delta Pi Society for *Religious Values and Peak-Experiences* by A.H.Maslow; Dr Mary Lambourne for permission to use material from a paper of the late Dr R.A. Lambourne; Penguin Books Ltd, for *The Birth and Death of Meaning* by Ernest Becker; Routledge and Kegan Paul Ltd, for *Modern Man in Search of a Soul* by C.G.Jung; also as publishers of *The British Journal of Sociology*, with Dr R.J.Bocock, for the latter's article 'The Symbolism of the Father'; SCM Press Ltd for *Basic Types of Pastoral Care and Counseling* by H.Clinebell, for *The Psychology of Religion* by H.Faber, and for *The Christian Neurosis* by

P.Solignac; the Rt Revd Dr Peter Selby for material from his paper; the Revd Dr Edward E. Thornton for the extracts from his *Theology and Pastoral Counseling*; the family of Dr Leslie Weatherhead for *Psychology, Religion and Healing*; Yale University Press for *Psychoanalysis and Religion* by Erich Fromm.

Every effort has been made to contact Drs William Clebsch and Charles R.Jaekle for *Pastoral Care in Historical Perspective* and Charles Scribner's Sons Ltd for *Insight* by J.Hillman. The editor would be glad to hear from the copyright holders of these two readings, so that due acknowledgement can be made in future editions of this book.

Introduction

Faith or fear? That question can be asked of several themes in this reader. Most obviously the psychological analysis of religion raises the issue whether faith is principally a negative response to the anxieties of living. Freud, for instance, suggests that religious faith is a reaction in the adult to fears about helplessness in the universe and in the face of death, parallel to a similar fear in the child of the actual power or phantasied omnipotence of parents. Similarly religious rituals, in Freud's view, are ways of trying to cope with fears coming from the 'inner world' – the unconscious. They are like obsessional rituals, ways of trying to contain dangerous impulses which threaten to overwhelm the conscious ego – the extract II:4 is a good example of this type of analysis.

There is ample evidence in religious practice to support such observations, although it has to be asked whether the hypothesis which Freud built upon such observations is either a conclusive or a comprehensive explanation of the significance of religious faith and practice. Every pastor could cite examples of those who use their religious faith defensively, to protect themselves (or sometimes in their evangelical zeal to protect others) from feelings which threaten their psychological equilibrium. 'Sin' becomes a euphemism for sexuality or aggression, and every measure is taken to reinforce the defences against such sins, without ever seeking to understand whether such feelings might be realized in more positive ways and so permit fuller, more mature relationships. The pastor could also point to other men and women of faith, who live with feelings of guilt which no gospel or sacrament of forgiveness ever seems to shift. The extracts II:8 and III:18 provide some examples of this type of fear-full or guilt-full faith.

The history of the Church is equally full of occasions when new theological ideas, exciting intellectual developments, and advances in ethical or scientific thinking, which could transform society or human relationships, have been repressed and their supporters ideologically or physically persecuted into submission, exile or death. Dogmas or rituals have at times been so protected

1

from intelligent criticism and treated as such sacred cows, that one might imagine that challenging them was to threaten the universe itself; yet one might also wonder what status such supposed truth had when it had to be protected in such inhuman ways. It is only institutions which are afraid of being exposed as inadequate, or which fear losing power and influence, that have to resort to oppression of a dissenter's faith. The extract II:9 draws such conclusions.

Yet such pictures are plainly one-sided. Faith coexists with fear, although faith seldom consists of fear alone. The history of the Church has many other facets which show the positive effects of religion; where, for instance, culture has been led into new heights of beauty and form by those whose inspiration comes from their religious faith; where ignorance and poverty have been the focus for concern, and where at least for a while the Church has taken the lead in combatting social evil; where principalities and powers have been rightly condemned and resisted for their oppression; and where it has frequently been the man or woman of faith who has been prepared to risk life itself in the pursuit of justice and truth. Two of the extracts from sociologists sympathetic to Freud (II:6 and II:7) also argue that religion has played a significant part in helping society control its inherent self-destructiveness and that modern Western society has not yet found a replacement for the faith which has been lost.

Here too the pastor can balance individual examples of neurotic faith with stories of those who give of themselves in a genuine concern for others and for the world, and who find self-fulfilment in doing so. He or she can point to those who, through the support of their faith, have not only been able to endure but even overcome the worst that life could throw at them; or indicate those whose capacity to survive negative experience has given them a faith which shines through their whole being and which has a magnetic effect even upon those who would normally scorn formal belief. Many of the extracts in Parts Two and Three recognize the positive contribution of religion to personal health and development (e.g. III:13–15), or the negative effects that come from the absence of faith (III:10). It is possible to distinguish between different expressions of faith, as in Fromm's definitions of authoritarian and humanitarian religion (III:12), or in Bloomfield's reminder of the existential distinction between authentic and inauthentic religion (III:18). In Parts Four and Five some of the readings demonstrate the value of religious faith as a guide to understanding a person's present life-position; and it appears that the development of faith can run parallel to the development

2

of the whole personality. If this is the case, and psychological development can lead to different faith-attitudes, perhaps it is also possible that greater pastoral concentration upon helping faith to mature could lead in turn to greater psychological maturity.

Faith or fear? Clearly both exist, inextricably bound up with each other, and probably in every religious person, albeit in different proportions. Even if faith is a response to human anxiety, this does not render faith redundant. Anxiety is endemic to the human condition, and if faith can provide ways of coping with that anxiety and so discourage people from retreating or from hiding from themselves or others, then faith and fear can co-exist in creative tension. Psychological explanations then serve more to describe the phenomenon of faith than to explain it away. So the Church need not be defensive about its institutional neuroticism, or that of its members; not because, in that overworn expression, it is a place for sinners, but because it was the critic Freud who himself demonstrated that neuroses are also the raw material through which important unconscious truth seeks expression. Fear may therefore be a starting point for deeper understanding of self and for growth towards greater maturity. What is important is that the Church continuously subjects itself to analysis of the possible psychological motives behind its pronouncements on faith, order and morals; and that religious men and women also have faith in the psychological method, so that they may use it as one of the ways of working towards a mature set of beliefs and values. Becker's words (III:16) suggest the potentialities for the mature use of faith: 'Religion itself is an ideal of strength and of potential for growth, of what man might become by assuming the burden of his life, as well as by being partly relieved of it.' The Freudian and post-Freudian age has contributed much to European culture and to our Western intellectual life. Psychoanalytic ideas may yet have as much to contribute to the development of faith as have other great intellectual movements to the laying down of our rich theological tradition.

'Faith or fear?' is also a question which can be asked about the one movement in the Church which has taken the psychological very much to heart, some would say too much to heart. Even though more widespread attention has been paid to pastoral counselling in Britain for over twenty years, the late eighties are seeing the spread of this interest amongst clergy and laity alike. The current fascination with this discipline partly reflects the general interest in counselling in the community at large. It is clearly a practical discipline, which has much to commend itself to the pastor who, if not approached for personal help on the scale of

3

the American pastor, nonetheless is surrounded, in middle-class parishes in particular, by obvious relationship crises. That a book of readings should be appeal to the interest in pastoral care and counselling will come as no surprise.

It is this fascination in, perhaps even the current obsession with, the psychological which raises other questions about faith or fear, which are addressed by some of the readings selected for this book. Does the interest in counselling disguise an anxiety about doing theology in the modern world? Or, equally important, does the fashion for counselling individuals serve as an escape from the equally essential gospel task of furthering the Kingdom of God? Is it easier than the challenging yet frustrating quest for social justice? Let us examine these two questions more closely.

It is certainly a major criticism of pastoral counselling that its concentration upon the individual, or the individual couple or family, and its use to resolve crises after they have occurred, tends towards the acceptance of or compliance with the social and economic conditions that cause or exacerbate the problems. Concern about individualism, and its corollary narcissism, can be found in several extracts (e.g. VI:30, VI:34–36). In much counselling, the individual is encouraged to concentrate upon her or his inner world. Counselling may well take place in a setting which deliberately distances the client from his home or place of work. Yet this may also be where part of the difficulty arises and in itself may appear to encourage people either to ignore reality, or to acquiesce in it. Pastoral counselling, somewhat like spiritual direction, tends to emphasize inner development rather than external change, leaving more prophetic and political voices to draw attention to the injustices of the social and economic order. Furthermore VI:31, for instance, reminds us of another reason why pastoral counselling cannot take place in isolation, because change in one individual can have a significant effect upon that person's family, or their environment. Pastoral counselling needs to be concerned with the whole, and not simply with the wholeness of the one.

Misplaced though such criticisms may appear to be to the pastoral counsellor, they are valid if the counsellor's particular expression of the significance of faith is confined to the inner world, or to values which cease the moment he or she leaves the counselling room. Most counsellors believe it is right to hold back from expression of their political, social and ethical views in counselling itself. Some pastoral counsellors would hold this to be just as necessary in respect of their religious views, although V:29 illustrates an alternative approach. It is the client's values, beliefs and phantasies that are important and interpretations will tend to concentrate upon psychological issues, not on political or social realities. Psychological maturity, of course, includes awareness of the wider dimensions of living in society, and the willingness to take risks and to act. However, many of the counsellor's clients find it difficult enough to find a personal sense of order, and are not initially concerned to do any more than survive the chaos they feel within. That the world about them is in turmoil would initially be felt only as a confirmation of their inner state. Theirs is a time in the wilderness, not yet ready to confront the world.

Pastoral counselling unfortunately (or perhaps fortunately – it really depends which way you look upon the process) takes up considerable time with few people, and is unlikely of itself to give rise to pressure movements. That does not stop counsellors themselves from raising political issues, which emerge from the work with their clients. Nor should the pastoral counsellor, in his or her concern for the inner world, look only to individual counselling for understanding. Group-work, particularly in parochial situations, may enable insight in the individual members of a group to be combined, at the right time, with facilitation of self-help and political activity. The sixties and seventies fashion in the Church for T-group training should remind us that individual counselling may have temporarily replaced that earlier enthusiasm for groupwork, but that the pastoral counsellor neglects that group-work experience at his or her peril. Furthermore, the combined skills and knowledge of the social psychologist and the pastoral counsellor forge a powerful tool for investigating some of the processes which take place within the national or local political arena. The pastor who wishes to work more on a community level than with individuals may nevertheless gain much from the pastoral counsellor's search for understanding of the unconscious processes in 'the principalities and powers'. To make a hard division between individual and group work is not good counselling practice, and to separate pastoral work in the community from pastoral work with individuals, as if the two had nothing in common or had nothing to give each other, is merely foolish.

At the same time I wonder what makes those, whose main emphasis in their pastoral work is on social and political involvement, come down as hard as they sometimes do on the pastoral counselling movement. While it is possible that faith in individual counselling can disguise fears of getting into the 'dirty and dangerous' games of politics, the pastoral counsellor can sometimes wonder whether the political Christian would rather deal with broad issues than be caught up in the anxious straits of the individual soul, or divide society into 'them' and 'us' rather than heal the split between good and bad in the innermost world. Authentic pastoral counselling is not a soft option. It is one thing to fear the arrow that flies by day, and to duck social responsibilities; it is another to fear the terrors of the night, and so ignore the terrifying underworld of the chaotic unconscious.

There is no simple answer to the many problems which arise from living, as we all have to, in two worlds at once. The external world clearly presents the religious person with problems of changing social and economic conditions. The inner world is just as difficult to change, and altering external circumstances is by no means always the answer. Yet there are common phrases which apply to both worlds, and which both the Christian counsellor and Christian community worker or politician would understand – one such phrase might be 'liberation'; another 'oppression'. In liberating people from oppression, the pastoral counsellor, and the pastoral community worker will no doubt adopt different methods, and insist upon different emphases. Yet each needs the other's contribution to the understanding of such terms, because while it is clear that many who come for counselling are also oppressed by the society in which they live, it is becoming equally evident that groups, small and large, including those which comprise society, can be understood as showing the same psychological phantasies and unconscious dynamics as any individual does. There is still a long way to go before such hypotheses about large groups can be applied constructively to society as a whole, but to separate the 'one' and the 'many' would be to weaken an important Old Testament concept which inextricably links the fortunes of the individual and his or her society. The inner world and the external world are complex enough in themselves to merit specialists in each area; but the specialisms need to meet and learn from each other if they are together to express the breadth of interpretation that must be given to the Kingdom of God, which is both 'in you' and in the world.

The other major question of faith or fear which I posed above was whether the current 'faith' in pastoral counselling masks the anxiety which today's pastor frequently has about her or his role in a secular world, which has little time for theological language. There is no doubt, despite the rearguard action of those who would introduce Test Acts for bishops, that theology is undergoing a crisis – see, for example, the extract III:17. That is, of course, nothing new; nor is a crisis a disaster. A crisis, as any pastoral counsellor can affirm, is an important opportunity for growth and

6

change; crises can even become exciting, particularly when one looks back on them and sees what they have helped forge. Yet any crisis is not pleasant when it starts, nor while it lasts, and it requires a particular kind of faith to stick with it, in the 'sure and certain hope' something valuable will eventually emerge from the confusion.

Pastoral counsellors, on the whole, are not theologians; whatever they have learned of theology in their past has given place to a new language, a specialized variant of psychology. Nevertheless, one has to ask whether such language has provided the pastor with a relatively easy escape from the tortuous task of re-evaluating theology in the pastoral (and of course the secular) setting? Or whether pastoral counselling has provided him or her with a role which makes her or him seem relevant at a time when for so many what the Church offers seems irrelevant? Guntrip asks such a question in extract IV:19. Following the latest fashion (and this applies equally to some other forms of pastoral concern such as the political) can be a way of avoiding the individual search for identity and authenticity. By submerging oneself in the values of the majority, the anomalies of faith and religion can be put to one side. Yet at the same time that which is most positive about faith and religion may be neglected.

I trust I am not unfair to pastoral counsellors. If I am, I am just as unfair to myself, and I write as I do to awaken them and myself to the exciting possibilities that exist for bringing theology to bear upon psychology, and psychology to bear upon theology. When the newer identity of the pastoral counsellor begins to consolidate (and it is doing that in Britain as, for instance, the Association for Pastoral Care and Counselling 'comes of age'), then it will be time to turn back to the theological resources – the extracts in Part One underline the concern which pastoral theologians have that pastoral counselling can lose sight of its theological parent – and engage in a quasi-incestuous relationship with the psychological parent. There is a division at present (fortunately far narrower than ten years ago) between those who teach pastoral studies and those who teach pastoral counselling – and probably therefore a theological, pastoral and practical dichotomy in those who learn from them.

I am not convinced that the theological resources will tell the pastoral counsellor anything which is startlingly new, but neither am I convinced that psychology really tells the pastor that either. Both disciplines tend rather to express for us that which we know, or (more accurately) believe already; there are of course as many varieties of theology just as there are of psychology, and we tend

7

towards those ideas in either discipline, which at any particular time reflect best what we feel (see V: 26). What is a more distinct possibility is that dialogue between pastoral counsellors and pastoral theologians (or those functions within the one person) will give rise to parallels in thinking in the two disciplines, each in its own way reflecting similar truths about persons. Subtle shades of expression, a little extra weight here, or a fraction of an angle there – those differences will surely exist. But ultimately, if there are points on which psychology and theology cannot agree, it is more probable that neither has got it right, rather than that one area should possess greater insight than the other.

Just as there are common phrases, such as those mentioned above, which link the individual and the community models of pastoral care, so there are a whole host of words upon which the theologian and pastoral counsellor could usefully reflect together: for example, original sin (the nature/nurture argument in psychology); actual sin (and the psychoanalytic idea that faults and errors are ways of achieving recognition of areas of potential growth); guilt (neurotic guilt, as well as realistic guilt, and the desire for reparation); atonement/at-one-ment (and the place of the counsellor in this process); forgiveness (from above or from within?); grace (and the internalized good object?); resurrection (and internalization of lost objects); omnipotence/idealization/divinization (of self and others); determinism and free-will (a psychological as well as a theological problem); spirit/soul (psyche), etc. This list is by no means exhaustive. The dialogue has hardly begun, and it may be fear of each other which prevents the sharing of the respective faiths and understandings of the pastoral counsellor, the pastoral prophet and the pastoral theologian. Hopefully the contributions in this reader, and their juxtaposition one with the other, may encourage that process forward.

MICHAEL JACOBS

Part I

The Tradition

I:1

The interest in the behavioural sciences, particularly psychology and sociology, which typifies our own era, is clear from the extensive literature by both secular and religious authors. This interest tends to obscure the long pastoral tradition in the Church, which from the ministry of Jesus and through the Fathers has spoken clearly to persons in need in every age, as well as to those who provide pastoral care. The language in which that tradition has spoken has been culture-linked, as much as is the terminology used in much current pastoral theology and practice. It has always reflected the knowledge (often from the humanities) known to those who wrote about the pastoral task, just as today's pastoral care and counselling writing and practice reflects the human sciences. Clebsch and Jaekle, have assembled a collection of readings, from the second Epistle of Clement through to William James, that more recent pioneer of the dialogue between faith and the newly emerging discipline of psychology; they remind us that we should not forget the wisdom of former times.

They also set out, in the introduction to their book, a definition of pastoral care which has been widely adopted amongst pastoral counsellors.[1] Ironically, Clebsch and Jaekle comment on the undue significance accorded to counselling, and predict that 'reconciling' will receive greater emphasis in the future. As later extracts show, their criticism of the stress on counselling has been echoed frequently since by different authors: and while 'reconciling' has indeed come to the fore in the pastoral care of society as a whole – particularly with their own stress on 'discipline', as in the criticism of society made by pastoral and liberation theologians – nonetheless counselling continues to attract perhaps disproportionate interest. This suggests that there is a further work of reconciliation to be done, in promoting a respectful and co-operative relationship

---

1. Their three terms, 'healing, sustaining and guiding' are also used by Seward Hiltner in his *Preface to Pastoral Theology* (Nashville, Abingdon Press, 1958) – an influential text, although better known in the United States than in Britain.

9

between two often quite distinct areas of pastoral concern (see particularly Section VI, and also my Introduction).

The Tradition of Pastoral Care[2]

Definitions

The ministry of the cure of souls, or pastoral care, consists of helping acts, done by *representative Christian persons,* directed toward the *healing, sustaining, guiding,* and *reconciling of troubled persons* whose troubles arise *in the context of ultimate meanings and concerns.*

I. *Representative Persons.* First and most simply, pastoral care is a ministry performed by *representative Christian persons,* persons who, either *de jure* or *de facto,* bring to bear upon human troubles the resources, the wisdom, and the authority of Christian faith and life. Such representative persons may or may not hold specific offices in a Christian church, although theirs is commonly the office of authorized pastors. . . .

II. *Troubled Persons.* Second, the ministry of pastoral care is directed to troubled persons and is aimed at supporting and helping them as individual persons. . . . Pastoral care begins when an individual person recognizes or feels that his trouble is insolvable in the context of his own private resources, and when he becomes willing, however subconsciously, to carry his hurt and confusion to a person who represents to him, however vaguely, the resources and wisdom and authority of religion.

Since soul care always deals with troubled persons, the pastor finds himself necessarily ready to support the individual against the claims of institutions and groups. Often between individual needs and institutional claims no antipathies arise, yet it is unrealistic and may even become cruel for the pastor to assume that they are always in harmony or are capable of being harmonized. Frequently pastoral care seeks to introduce an individual into a group in order to relieve his hurt or even in order to place him in the way of finding relief. When that introduction is undertaken, however, *for the sake of the group, pastoral care ceases* and some other ministry, perhaps that of evangelization, begins. . . .

V. *Functions of pastoral care.* Each special function of the cure of souls calls for brief description.

A. HEALING is that function in which a representative Christian

2. From W. A. Clebsch, C. R. Jaekle, *Pastoral Care in Historical Perspective* (New Jersey, Prentice-Hall, 1964), pp. 4–10, 79–82. See also J. T. McNeill, *A History of the Cure of Souls.* New York, Harper and Row, 1951.

person helps a debilitated person to be restored to a condition of wholeness, on the assumption that this restoration achieves also a new level of spiritual insight and welfare. Pastoral healing, thus, involves recuperation from a specific ill, but it is distinguished by the fact that it regards cures as advancements in the soul's ability to reckon on illness and health as experiences fraught with spiritual significance. . . .

B. SUSTAINING consists of helping a hurting person to endure and to transcend a circumstance in which restoration to his former condition or recuperation from his malady is either impossible or so remote as to seem improbable. The sustaining function normally employs the means of compassionate commiseration. But it goes beyond mere resignation to affirmation as it attempts to achieve spiritual growth through endurance of unwanted or harmful or dangerous experiences. Perhaps the commonest form of sustaining is found in the pastoral ministry to bereaved persons, whose loss is indeed unredeemable but whose experience opens up the significant spiritual implications of death as confronting the bereaved and as having confronted the deceased.

C. The pastoral function of GUIDING consists of assisting perplexed persons to make confident choices between alternative courses of thought and action, when such choices are viewed as affecting the present and future state of the soul. Guidance commonly employs two identifiable modes. *Eductive guidance* tends to draw out of the individual's own experiences and values the criteria and resources for such decisions, while *inductive guidance* tends to lead the individual to adopt an *a priori* set of values and criteria by which to make his decision. Perhaps the most familiar modern form of eductive guidance is that commonly known as 'client-centered therapy', while inductive guidance classically appeals to the long tradition of Christian moral theology and casuistry.

D. The RECONCILING function seeks to re-establish broken relationships between man and fellow man and between man and God. Broadly speaking, each of these horizontal and vertical relationships has been understood as inescapably involving the other. That is to say, while we may distinguish between broken or restored relationships with God and with neighbor, only very rarely has Christian pastoring dared to separate them. Reconciling employs two emphatic modes of operation, which we call forgiveness and discipline. . . .

It must be remarked that in various times and places the *means* which have been employed by these various functions, even in their various modes, have changed and shifted greatly. *Healing*,

11

for example, has employed such instrumentalities as prayer, oil, herbs, medicines, relics, shrines, words of exorcism, vows, and so forth. *Sustaining* has also used prayer, holy objects, regulations, and so on . . . *Guiding* has employed many different techniques of counseling, and has appealed to various codifications of virtues and sins, manuals of advice, and the like. *Reconciling* has employed various sacramental, ritual, and personal means.

Emergence of a New Era?

. . . a new epoch of pastoral activity is about to emerge from our present time of transition. Evidence of an emerging era dominated by reconciling can be found, but this evidence supports no clear and unequivocal prognostication. There appears a picture made up of blurred outlines, outlines that may be painted over by subsequent shifts and movements in the helping professions. Such as they are, these outlines embolden us to dare set down what we see as indications for the immediate future of pastoring under Christian auspices. Sustaining seems the most widely practiced of the pastoral functions. Guiding seems at present to engender a fascination disproportionate to its promise for the future. Reconciling seems to gain a prominence that might allow it to polarize the other functions. Healing seems capable of recrudescence under the sponsorship of reconciling. The tentativeness of these predictions is proportionate to their brevity.

The sustaining function of the cure of souls in our day continues to be a crucially important helping ministry, sufficiently versatile to be adapted to circumstances of urban-industrial living. Everywhere today busy pastors are called upon to sustain troubled persons in, through, and beyond a plethora of hurts that brook no direct restoration. In terms of time and emotional energy, perhaps of all the pastoral functions sustaining demands most from ordained clergymen. Several reasons can be adduced to explain the continuing viability of this function. The mobility of persons in modern societies has torn the fabric of neighborly relations that recently helped people withstand devastating disruptions of living. . . .

Despite the present-day practical importance of sustaining, guiding as a pastoral function seems to command highest attention in our time. A rich and varied literature on pastoral counseling is available to clergy during their professional preparation and practice. Opportunities for clinical training in hospitals and counseling centers stimulate critical reflection about, and provide competent supervision over, pastoral counseling. During recent years, counseling has been the chief locus of concern for pastoral theology and pastoral psychology. Even while sustaining may have demanded more of the pastor's time and energy than other functions, counseling has become the gate through which new intellectual formulations of pastoring have entered and claimed attention. In part this emphasis upon counseling has arisen from religion's twin needs to digest the theoretical formulations that arise from psychiatry and psychology, and to utilize this theory in pastoral helping. Broadly speaking, the dominant mode of recent helping activity has been what we have called individually eductive guiding, and undoubtedly the most provocative research and writing about the helping professions have concentrated upon counseling. The vast majority of training opportunities for clergy, meanwhile, have been under auspices of institutions whose central concern was counseling as the chief model of the helping art.

The very fact that pastoral guiding has become fascinating insofar as it became subsidiary to the other helping arts seems to indicate that the current interest in pastoral counseling, however valuable in other ways, holds little promise as a pole around which the entire pastoral ministry may be magnetized. We see more creative opportunities in another direction; namely the ministry of reconciling. This function, closely allied with but dominating the function of healing, appears on the verge of an important revival. In spite of the fact that reconciling, in both modes of forgiveness and discipline, has suffered recent neglect, it remains in heavy demand. We foresee in the resuscitation of the reconciling function, synthesized with that of healing, the best hope for a transformed pastoral care that is at once continuous with the history of pastoring, integrated with the churches' theological formulations, open to new psychological insights, and able to meet creatively the aspirations and needs of modern men and women.

The reconciling function enjoys an extraordinarily rich heritage in the church and remains a manner of helping for which there is, as yet, no prominent non-pastoral substitute. The burden of guilt under which moderns live – guilt engendered by alienation from fellow man that interprets itself as also alienation from God – is a form of human trouble with which the pastoral ministry has had longer and deeper familiarity than has any other helping profession. Partly by virtue of insisting that broken human relationships involve a breach in man's ultimate relationship with his Creator, pastoral care takes the human need for reconciliation with a seriousness unsurpassed by that of other healing arts. Urban mobility and the consequent shifting of patterns of family life have exacerbated parents' guilt over their children, and, later on, children's guilt over the problem of responsibility for aging

13

parents. Lacking the protection of well-patterned and stable expectations, modern marriage throws husbands and wives into situations where more and more arise questions and burdens and inadequacies in their responsibilities to one another. Thus, the related matters of guilt, responsibility, relationship, alienation, and reconcilation comprise a genus of modern human trouble for which the reconciling ministry is peculiarly well suited.

Reconciling persons who suffer from ruptured relationships is an aim woven into the very fabric of the church's liturgy and theology as well as its pastoral care. It is natural that the clergyman among representatives of the helping arts is most expected to be peacemaker and reconciler. That the clergy are so very frequently turned to by persons with marital difficulties involving relationships with spouses and by persons with other problems of human relationships occasions no surprise. To him alienated persons confess their yearnings and ambivalences and even hatreds in sure knowledge that their attitudes will be both judged and forgiven, and in the hope that their relationships will be reconciled. His ritual functions of baptizing, of declaring God's forgiveness of sin, of solemnizing matrimony, and so forth, both announce and renew his authority as a person peculiarly concerned with establishing and restoring relationships of profound significance between man and man and between man and God.

Pastoral reconciling finds a natural connection today with pastoral healing, because, in the Christian vision of life, restored relationships not only achieve a *status quo ante* but represent a spiritual advance with relationships that have never suffered breaches. This characteristic of Christian pastoral reconciling suits the mood of modern man for personal growth and his expectation that the whole of one's life in relationship to others will be characterized by the increasing release of one's creative powers.

I:2

One particularly strong reaction against the current baptism by immersion of pastoral counselling in secular psychotherapy comes from Thomas Oden. Over many years he has himself been continuously and thoroughly involved in what has proved to be a circuitous dialogue with the 'richness and limitations' of psychotherapy. He has written extensively on the integration of theology and therapy. In a major U-turn in the seventies, Oden became aware of 'the dubious effectiveness of average psychotherapy'; and since then he has tried to recover the classical pastoral tradition. In an article

14

which prefigures a major book, 'Pastoral Theology' (see 1:3), he traces his pilgrimage; and then analyses a range of influential texts used in nineteenth- and twentieth-century pastoral theology. He selected ten key figures in classical pastoral care, and found 164 references to them in the seven nineteenth-century writers. However he found no references whatsoever to them in his seven representative twentieth-century writers. By contrast he found 330 references in the latter to contemporary psychotherapists. He comments:

Recovering Lost Identity [3]

What happened after 1920? It is as if a great pendulum gradually reverses its direction and begins to swing the other way. A key figure in the reversal was Anton Boisen, the founder of the clinical pastoral education movement, a creative man in whom the classical tradition still lived and whose works are still eminently worth reading. Pastoral care soon acquired a consuming interest in psychoanalysis, psychopathology, clinical methods of treatment, and in the whole string of therapeutic approaches that were to follow Freud. It was a vital and significant problematic, but regrettably the theological moorings were not sufficient to prevent an ever increasing amnesia toward the previous traditions of pastoral counseling. It is as if a giant shade were pulled and pulled rather quickly. What has occurred subsequently are wave after wave of various hegemonies of emergent psychologies accommodated cheaply into pastoral care without much self-conscious identity formation from the tradition. I do not want to exaggerate so as to suggest that the classical tradition of pastoral care was entirely forgotten. That did not happen. We are still living out of it implicitly, because social patterns and historical paradigms are maintained at grass roots levels by resilient social traditioning despite changing ideologies and leadership elites. But the classical tradition had not been diligently *studied* since the 1920s. We are now at the far end of that pendulum swing, and the momentum is again reversing.

During the past twenty years of my professional life, the methodological key to the active energies of pastoral care has been its pervasive eros[4] toward the accommodation of various therapies from orthodox Freudian and Jungian all the way through the spectrum of Sullivan, Rogers, Skinner, Fromm, Perls, Berne,

3. From T. C. Oden, 'Recovering Lost Identity' (*The Journal of Pastoral Care*, vol. XXXIV, no. 1, March 1980, pp. 4–19).
4. i.e. a love-affair with (Ed.).

Ellis, Schultz, etc., etc., etc. – all of these one by one have been courted and accommodated (often rather uncritically) *to* the structures, language and professional apparatus of Christian ministry. Thus the task of the 'pastoral counselor' thus understood in recent years has tended to become that of trying to ferret out what is currently happening or likely to happen next in the sphere of emergent psychology and adapting it as deftly as possible to the work of ministry, but in the adaptation the fundament of Christian pastoral care in its classical sense is neglected at best and at worst polemicized. So pastoral theology has become in many cases little more than an accommodation to the most current psychological trends (often, as psychologist Paul Vitz has astutely shown, a pop expression of a bad psychology to begin with), with only the slenderest accountability to the classical pastoral tradition. Meanwhile it is little wonder that the working pastor continues to look in vain to the field of pastoral theology for some distinction between Christian pastoral care and pop psych faddism. I may be exaggerating slightly, but I think not much. . . .

The Promise of an Enriched Synthesis Between Old and New

Finally it seems fitting to speak, even if tentatively, of the challenge and promise of the road ahead for us in Christian pastoral care, assuming a new accessibility to the tradition. I am not proposing a reactionary archaism that would rigidly repeat past culturally determined formulae. The task that lies ahead is the development of a post-modern post-Freudian, neo-classical approach to Christian pastoral care which has taken seriously the resources of modernity, but which has also penetrated its illusions, and having found the best of modern psychotherapies still problematic, has turned again to the classical tradition for its bearings, yet without disowning what it has learned from modern clinical experience.

In order to do this, we must learn in some fresh new way the courage to give intelligent resistance to the narcissistic imperialism and hedonistic reductionism that prevails both in the culture and to a certain extent also in the churches. This courage I have not yet seen, but nothing is more crucial for us in this field than to find its ground and possibility. We can no longer afford ourselves the luxury of allowing contemporary psychotherapies to define for us what pastoral care is. We must define for ourselves again what pastoral care is, and in what sense pastoral theology is and remains theology. Otherwise more wheel-spinning and professional identity confusion.

The task is not merely that of giving critical resistance to present trends, but more so of giving new energies to a wholesome recon-struction of a pastoral care that is informed by Christian theology, able to provide a credible pastoral theodicy, aware of the dialectic of grace and freedom, gospel and law, and able to point saliently to the providence of God amid our human alienations.

But *really*, you ask, what can the classical tradition usefully contribute to modern pastoral counseling? What practical differ-ence might it make if it were taken seriously, while at the same time we were trying to hold on to the achievements of contem-porary clinically-oriented pastoral care? Although it is far too early to answer these questions with any certainty, here are some of the general shifts of direction that I would expect to occur, to a greater or lesser degree.

1. Pastoral *intercessory prayer* would again become an important aspect of pastoral interaction.

2. The *antinomianism* of contemporary pastoral care (under the influence of pop psychologies) would be more effectively resisted by a more balanced dialectic of gospel and law.

3. Marriage counseling would tend to function more within the framework of the traditional Christian doctrine of *matrimony* rather than esssentially as a hedonic cost/benefit calculus.

4. *Empathy* training for pastoral counseling would be more deliberately and self-consciously grounded in an incarnational understanding of God's participation in human alienation.

5. Out of our recent history of exaggerated self-expression, feeling disclosure and narcissism, we may be in for a new round of experimentation in *askesis*, self-discipline, self-denial and rigorism which might in turn threaten to become exaggerated in a maso-chistic direction, and thus again need the corrective of a balanced Christian anthropology.

6. The diminishing moral power of the previously prevailing momentum of individualistic autonomy and self-assertiveness may call for a new emphasis in group process upon corporate responsi-bility, mutual accountability, *moral self-examination*, and social commitment that would be undergirded by studies in Bible and tradition.

7. We are ready for a new look at the traditional Protestant pattern of regular pastoral *visitation*, which could enter many doors now closed to most secular therapists.

8. Pastoral visitation and counseling would work harder than it is now working to develop a thorough and meaningful *pastoral theodicy* that takes fully into account the philosophical and moral objections to classical Christian arguments on the problem of evil

and the meaning of suffering, yet with new attentiveness to the deeper pastoral intent of that tradition.

9. The new synthesis will interweave evangelical *witness* more deliberately into the process of pastoral conversation rather than disavowing witness or disassociating proclamation from therapeutic dialogue.

10. *Group experimentation* would continue, but be rooted more awarely in classical Christian understandings of *koinonia, marturia* and *diakonia*.

11. Older therapeutic approaches such as fasting, dietary control, meditation, and concrete acts of restitution are likely to have new importance.

12. The now atrophied concept of '*call to ministry*' may need to be thoroughly restudied, and reconceived as a hinge concept of the pastoral office, and of ordination.

13. Contemporary pastoral theology in dialogue with the classical tradition may learn to speak *amen* in a rigorous way about the spiritual and moral qualifications for ministry, reflecting the tradition's concern for moral character, humility, zeal, and self-denial.

14. The modern pastor may learn to adapt to contemporary interactions something of the finely atuned and sensitive *art of spiritual direction* as developed in the classical tradition.

15. Pastoral care will become less prone to messianism faddism, because it would have built into it a critical apparatus more deeply rooted in the Christian tradition.

16. A non-sexist, non-chauvinist reinterpretation of ministry, prayer, pastoral care and spiritual direction will require a serious critical dialogue with tradition, a dialogue that must be as far-ranging as the radical feminists assert, and yet able to listen carefully to the collective wisdom of Christian historical experience; that critical dialogue is worth risking, and far better than a simplistic accommodation to modern individualistic narcissism or reductive naturalisms.

17. The term pastoral counseling will again be reclaimed as an integral part of the pastoral office, intrinsically correlated with liturgy, preaching, and the nurture of Christian community, and relatively less identified with purely secularized, non-ecclesial, theologically emasculated fee basis counseling.

1:3

Oden's 'Pastoral Theology' spells out his argument in greater detail. In his review of the book, John Elford, a pastoral theologian at

Manchester University, asks three major questions, the second of which justifiably corrects the American emphasis (not just in Oden) on pastoral counselling as almost exclusively a function of the ordained ministry. To be fair, there are American writers (some of whom have witnessed the number of lay people involved in pastoral counselling in Britain) who are asking the same question. Oden's emphasis on shepherding as a main function of ministry is again typical of his compatriots, following Seward Hiltner and others in assigning a more directive quality to the role than is traditionally understood in Britain.

A Response to Oden [5]

During the twentieth century Christian pastoral theology has, according to Thomas Oden, lost its identity. This is because it has been too uncritically preoccupied with modern psychoanalytic approaches to human welfare – approaches which Oden himself writes about, often more sympathetically, in some of his earlier works. . . . *Pastoral Theology* marks a change of mind by its author, about much that he has previously taken for granted, a change that was signalled by his article: 'Recovering Lost Identity'. . . .

What Oden is now at pains to make clear is something which Christian pastors should generally welcome. Unless we know what constitutes the identity of Christian pastoral theology then we will not be able to cope with modernity without either; a) ignoring it irresponsibly, or b) embracing it uncritically. In *Pastoral Theology* Oden returns, again and again, to Christian tradition in order to discover the historic identity of pastoral theology. No small part of the value of this work lies in the extensive bibliographies he assembles for this purpose and appends to each chapter.

The book is about ministry. This is because it defines pastoral theology as ' . . . that branch of Christian Theology that deals with the office, gifts and functions of the pastor' (p. 311). More sharply put: pastoral theology is ministerial territory which sees that ' . . . a major part of the task ahead (of it) is to sharpen anew the needed distinction between clergy and laity' (p. 3). These rather stark definitions give rise to at least two questions.

Firstly, is pastoral theology only about what ministers do? So defined, it becomes dangerously relegated to the periphery of

5. Review article by R. John Elford of *Pastoral Theology* by T.C. Oden, San Francisco, Harper and Row, 1983 (*Contact*, 86, 1985, pp. 25–7).

theological activity; the practical bit, or what you study when you want to apply theology to human welfare. Such a definition of pastoral theology is not itself new. It is often described as 'practical theology', as though the terms were synonymous. But they are not. There is much more to pastoral theology than this. Indeed, it can be argued that pastoral theology is the foundation of all theology. So understood it is the study of the reasons why theology, as a human activity, needs to be undertaken at all – reasons which have to do with the greatness of human need in the face of overwhelming difficulties and perplexities. Countless examples of this could be given; of ways, that is, in which perceptions of such need have inspired and even changed the direction of theology itself. Two such perceptions illustrate the point. St Augustine wrote his *City of God* as an apologia for Christianity. It turned out to be nothing less than a treatise on the nature and destiny of humankind, which was made necessary by the sack of Rome by Alaric and the Goths in 410 AD. His perception of the pastoral needs created by this momentous event created a new sort of theology. In more recent times, Karl Barth wrote his *Epistle to the Romans*, because the sufferings of the First World War had seriously challenged the historical pretensions of Liberal Protestantism. The impact on subsequent theology of both these examples is well known. What they illustrate, for our purpose, is the way in which pastoral need is often the most profound spring for creative theological activity. Liberation theology is yet another obvious, latter-day example. To press the point: it may be claimed that the history of theology, with which Oden is rightly concerned, counts against his narrow definition of what pastoral theology is about.

Secondly, do we really need to sharpen anew the needed distinction between clergy and laity? Oden's main reason for thinking that we do, seems to arise from the laudable concern to emphasise the professionalism of the clergy. But even if that is a proper concern, is this the way to achieve it? Oden implies, as he does in his definition of pastoral theology, that the clergy are professional because they possess, exclusively, a corpus of knowledge to which other people have no access. Such a definition of professionalism is common among the secular professions. Medicine is an obvious example. It is not appropriate to the Christian ministry. Whatever might be meant by calling that ministry professional, it cannot be implied that it is so because clergy know things which the laity cannot, by definition, also know. Oden does address himself to the question of equipping the laity for ministry, but interestingly only devotes 16 of his 372 pages to this end. Furthermore, most of these few pages are concerned with how the laity are to be 'organized' by the clergy. He does allow that the laity have a role in ministry, but, unlike that of the clergy, it is not a 'representative' one. All this tacitly presupposes that, by virtue of their superior knowledge, the clergy exercise an authority over the laity in pastoral matters. They are the strong shepherds who care for and direct the weak sheep. This is dangerous. It relegates the pastoral care of the laity (which means by far the greater part of all pastoral care), to a subordinate role. The greater truth is that all Christian pastoral care is representative for the simple reason that it represents Him in whose name it is carried out. All should care for the souls of all, and all Christian care is equal in the sight of God.

These are important questions to ask of the book since they challenge two of its fundamental presuppositions. There is still a further and more general question to ask.

Oden is, as I have said, rightly concerned to relate contemporary Christian pastoral theology to Christian tradition. What he either does or comes very close to doing, is to treat that tradition as though it can be understood quite apart from modernity; as though, that is, Freud and Jung had never done their work. Our perceptions of tradition are constantly changing. This is why it has to be studied continuously. What we can never do is to produce a timeless exposition of tradition which will serve regardless of our own experiences and changing knowledge. There is no point in understanding the past if we have to abandon the present in order to do it. Oden is aware that this criticism may be made of his book and, in some ways he refutes it, by citing his earlier works, as I have mentioned above. But the reader is still left with wondering how to use the knowledge of the past, which Oden authoritatively assembles, in the light of her or his experience of the present. Oden's approach thus raises important questions about how we understand the past and how we use that knowledge in the present. His solution to this question, which is in effect to ignore the present, will not convince many, disillusioned though they may rightly be with aspects of modernity.

Part II

The Psychological Critique of Faith and Religion

II:4

Sigmund Freud needs little introduction; and although Jung's writing probably attracts more sympathy from Christians, Freud's analysis of religion cannot be ignored. He was, of course, not the first to suggest that religion meets the need for a parental figure; Feuerbach, for instance, had said the same earlier in the nineteenth century. Nor is Freud's serious critique lacking in support from Christian writing since. There have been attempts to dismiss his arguments by pointing to reasons for his hostility to religion (and Catholicism in particular), by analysing his own life experiences. Such efforts only serve to substantiate his main argument, that God and religious symbolism act as a blank screen upon which we project fears and wishes from early experience, or from phantasied experience of our parents. Freud wrote several books on religion (such as 'Totem and Taboo' *(1912–13),* 'The Future of an Illusion' *(1928) and* 'Moses and Monotheism' *(1939)); but some of his material is seriously questionable in the light of biblical criticism and field anthropology. An earlier paper concentrates more upon his real field of expertise, the individual patient, and hence carries more weight. In the light of later Freudian and post-Freudian writing, it is possible for the reader to substitute the words 'feeling, emotion' or his own word 'impulse' for the now more questionable use of the term 'instinct', in order to clarify Freud's explanation of obsessional behaviour. It is also important to add that Freud recognized, of course, the restraints put upon expression of feeling which living in society may require, and saw no easy answer to the problem.*

Obsessive Actions and Religious Practices [1]

I am certainly not the first person to have been struck by the resemblance between what are called obsessive actions in sufferers

1. From S. Freud, *Obsessive Actions and Religious Practices,* 1907 (London, Hogarth Press, 1959 [Standard Edition, vol. ix] pp. 115–27; and Pelican Freud Library, 1985 [vol. 13] pp. 31–41).

from nervous affections and the observances by means of which believers give expression to their piety. . . .

Neurotic ceremonials consist in making small adjustments to particular everyday actions, small additions or restrictions or arrangements, which have always to be carried out in the same, or in a methodically varied, manner. These activities give the impression of being mere formalities, and they seem quite meaningless to us. Nor do they appear otherwise to the patient himself; yet he is incapable of giving them up, for any deviation from the ceremonial is visited by intolerable anxiety, which obliges him at once to make his omission good. Just as trivial as the ceremonial actions themselves are the occasions and activities which are embellished, encumbered and in any case prolonged by the ceremonial – for instance, dressing and undressing, going to bed or satisfying bodily needs. The performance of a ceremonial can be described by replacing it, as it were, by a series of unwritten laws . . . in slight cases the ceremonial seems to be no more than an exaggeration of an orderly procedure that is customary and justifiable; but the special conscientiousness with which it is carried out and the anxiety which follows upon its neglect stamp the ceremonial as a 'sacred act'. Any interruption of it is for the most part badly tolerated, and the presence of other people during its performance is almost always ruled out. . . .

It is easy to see where the resemblances lie between neurotic ceremonials and the sacred acts of religious ritual: in the qualms of conscience brought on by their neglect, in their complete isolation from all other actions (shown in the prohibition against interruption) and in the conscientiousness with which they are carried out in every detail. But the differences are equally obvious, and a few of them are so glaring that they make the comparison a sacrilege: the greater individual variability of (neurotic) ceremonial actions in contrast to the stereotyped character of rituals (prayer, turning to the East, etc.), their private nature as opposed to the public and communal character of religious observances, above all, however, the fact that, while the minutiae of religious ceremonial are full of significance and have a symbolic meaning, those of neurotics seem foolish and senseless. In this respect an obsessional neurosis presents a travesty, half comic and half tragic, of a private religion. But it is precisely this sharpest difference between neurotic and religious ceremonial which disappears when, with the help of the psychoanalytic technique of investigation, one penetrates to the true meaning of obsessive actions. In the course of such an investigation the appearance which obsessive actions afford of being foolish and senseless is

23

completely effaced, and the reason for their having that appearance is explained. It is found that the obsessive actions are perfectly significant in every detail, that they serve important interests of the personality and that they give expression to experiences that are still operative and to thoughts that are cathected with affect. . . .

[*Here Freud provides clinical examples to illustrate his argument. – Ed.*]

A deeper insight into the mechanism of obsessional neurosis is gained if we take into account the primary fact which lies at the bottom of it. This is always *the repression of an instinctual impulse* (a component of the sexual instinct) which was present in the subject's constitution and which was allowed to find expression for a while during his childhood but later succumbed to suppression. In the couse of the repression of this instinct a special *conscientiousness* is created which is directed against the instinct's aims; but this psychical reaction-formation feels insecure and constantly threatened by the instinct which is lurking in the unconscious. . . . Thus the ceremonial and obsessive actions arise partly as a defence against the temptations and partly as a protection against the ill which is expected. . . . A further characteristic of obsessional neurosis, as of all similar affections, is that its manifestions (its symptoms, including the obsessive actions) fulfil the condition of being a compromise between the warring forces of the mind. They thus always reproduce something of the pleasure which they are designed to prevent; they serve the repressed instinct no less than the agencies which are repressing it. . . .

Some features of this state of affairs may be seen in the sphere of religious life as well. The formation of a religion, too, seems to be based on the suppression, the renunciation, of certain instinctual impulses. These impulses, however, are not, as in the neuroses, exclusively components of the sexual instinct; they are self-seeking, socially harmful instincts, though, even so, they are usually not without a sexual component. A sense of guilt following upon continual temptation and an expectant anxiety in the form of fear of divine punishment have, after all, been familiar to us in the field of religion longer than in that of neurosis. Perhaps because of the admixture of sexual components, perhaps because of some general characteristics of the instincts, the suppression of instinct proves to be an inadequate and interminable process in religious life also. Indeed, complete backslidings into sin are more common among pious people than among neurotics and these give rise to a new form of religious activity, namely acts of penance, which have their counterpart in obsessional neurosis.

. . . the petty ceremonials of religious practice gradually become the essential thing and push aside the underlying thoughts. That is why religions are subject to reforms which work retroactively and aim at a re-establishment of the original balance of values. . . .

In view of these similarities and analogies one might venture to regard obsessional neurosis as a pathological counterpart of the formation of a religion, and to describe that neurosis as an individual religiosity and religion as a universal obsessional neurosis.

II:5

The brief extract which follows, from the correspondence between Freud and the Swiss Protestant pastor Oscar Pfister, introduces the hint of a more positive attitude in Freud. The possibility of dialogue between psychoanalysis and religion is shown in their own friendship, Pfister wrote a reply to 'The Future of an Illusion' in his own 'The Illusion of a Future'. (For a paper on, and extensive bibliography of, Pfister's writing, see 'The Journal of Pastoral Care', vol. xxxv, no. 4, December, 1981, pp. 220–39.)

Godless Jew? [2]

As for the possibility of sublimation to religion, therapeutically I can only envy you. But the beauty of religion certainly does not belong to psycho-analysis. It is natural that at this point in therapy our ways should part, and so it can remain. Incidentally, why was it that none of all the pious ever discovered psycho-analysis? Why did it have to wait for a completely godless Jew?

With cordial greetings from
Your old friend Freud

PFISTER TO FREUD   *Zürich,*
29.10.1918

. . . Finally you ask why psycho-analysis was not discovered by

2. From H. Meng, and E. L. Freud, *Psychoanalysis and Faith: The Letters of Sigmund Freud and Oscar Pfister* (London, Hogarth Press, 1963), p. 63.

any of the pious, but by an atheist Jew. The answer obviously is that piety is not the same as genius for discovery and that most of the pious did not have it in them to make such discoveries. Moreover, in the first place you are no Jew, which to me, in view of my unbounded admiration for Amos, Isaiah, Jeremiah, and the author of Job and Ecclesiastes, is a matter of profound regret, and in the second place you are not godless, for he who lives the truth lives in God, and he who strives for the freeing of love 'dwelleth in God' (First Epistle of John, iv, 16). If you raised to your consciousness and fully felt your place in the great design, which to me is as necessary as the synthesis of the notes is to a Beethoven symphony, I should say of you: A better Christian there never was. . . .

II:6

A more recent, yet traditionally Freudian, analysis of the development of religion in cultural context is found in Badcock's 'Psychoanalysis of Culture'. This fascinating study of religion, from animism to Catholicism, interprets ethological, anthropological and theological data in the light of Freud's use of the theory of the primal horde (see II:7) – despite this theory being criticized by many authoritative social scientists. Badcock extends Freud's thesis of the universal neurosis in religion and culture. In his conclusion, Badcock acknowledges the value to society of the flowering of post-Renaissance Catholicism, but only as a step on the way towards his claim that it is psychoanalysis that represents the true maturing of the religious quest: indeed he is in danger of repeating Freud's occasionally expressed desire that psychoanalysis should become the coping-stone of science and culture. Despite this tendency to claim more for psychoanalysis than it can bear, the use of the traditionally Freudian parallel between the development of the individual and the development of religion and culture in society merits attention, as long as the temptation to turn psychoanalysis into a yet another comprehensive religious system can be resisted.

The Return of the Repressed in Religion [3]

. . . it is the nature of psychoanalysis and its commitment to the reality principle that it should make possible the fullest imaginable

3. From C. R. Badcock, *The Psychoanalysis of Culture* (Oxford, Blackwell, 1980), pp. 248–53.

26

return of the repressed and the most complete abreaction of latent emotions.

It is in this respect that psychoanalysis is formally comparable to a return of Catholicism. Catholicism has been aptly named, for it really does contain every aspect of religion considered in these pages. In so far as it is a re-embodiment of classical polytheism, it contains all that polytheism did, namely, vestiges of totemism, a great deal of animism and magic, phallic earth-goddesses, and the divine kings who were the male gods of polytheism. In so far as it was an off-shoot of Jewish monotheism, Catholicism also contains both the punitive monotheism of pastoralism and the paranoid, providential monotheism of Egypt. In short, it holds within itself all the major elements of all that went before it: animism, totemism, polytheism, and monotheism. As the last term in the evolution of the sequence of religions studied here and the final exorcism of the idea of God, psychoanalysis is the most complete revelation of what is real in religion and therefore must be something as comprehensive – as *catholic* – in its scope as Catholicism. It corresponds to the ultimate stage in man's emancipation from the past and from the neurosis of religion, and so must also entail a comprehensive abreaction of the ambivalences on which the neurosis was originally built.

In the richness and diversity of its ritual and belief no religion has ever surpassed Catholicism. The reason is clear: Catholicism contained something to gratify every aspect of man's mind. He could call on the saints to satisfy his latent animism; he could attend the totem-feast of the Mass and gratify his Oedipal ambivalences; he could pray to the Virgin in order to sublimate his incestuous love for his mother; he could fear God the Father to gratify his conscience. In its almost inexhaustible religious riches Catholicism could be all things to all men. . . .

Yet is is inevitable that if psychoanalysis is to succeed in being the final resolution of man's neurosis it will have to shift its main interest away from individual psychotherapy towards education and applied social psychology . . . the young would have to be equipped with symbolic means of acting-out their ambivalences and advancing their mastery of themselves. But where would such symbolism come from? If the principal argument of this book is correct, there exists a deep and significant analogy between the history of the individual as reflected in his psychology and that of the entire human race as reflected in its religion. Each and every one of us who makes the transition from birth to maturity success- fully recapitulates within himself the entire past of his species and

27

marks in the stages of his psychic development the great turning-points in the history of humanity. As a new-born baby he is living in the state of primal narcissism and, like our distant foraging ancestors, still at one with nature, still totally preoccupied with feeding, still innocent of inhibition and untouched by neurosis. As a child of three he is developing totemism, lusting like his early hunting ancestors after the flesh of the mother and plotting like them the death of the father. By the age of five the Oedipal crisis is passing and he is in a transitional stage comparable to polytheism in which he is totemist, animist, worshipper of the phallic mother, and monotheist by turns. At the beginning of the period he believed that the mother had a penis of her own just as in the early days of agriculture women symbolically possessed one when they impregnated Mother Earth with the first domesticated seeds. Later the phallic goddess of agriculture was castrated and replaced by the male gods of polytheism, just as the young child eventually sees his mother as castrated and replaced by his father who now becomes the parent with whom he identifies and on whom he builds his super-ego. When this process is complete, at about six or seven, he is a monotheist who cannot admit that he feels anything but love for the totem-father of his earlier days; the super-ego develops its punitive powers to the full and latency supervenes. As puberty begins, he lives through the early history of Christianity; he becomes a new St Paul, and sublimates his adolescent homosexuality in the ascetic charity of St Francis, or intellectualizes like a latter day Thomas Aquinas. But sometimes he succumbs to the insistent demands of his newly aroused id and becomes a medieval troubadour, obsessed with love and with being loved, the incurable erotic who alternates with the austere ascetic. Later, he relives the Reformation in his egoistic confrontations with his father who ineluctably becomes the Pope and Holy Roman Emperor against whom the tide of history has already turned. Gradually, as the insolent self-assertiveness of adolescence passes and the reality principle gains the upper hand, he is ready to rediscover psychoanalysis and to realize that his ego is secure and can face up to his unconscious without fear. . . . No other education could be superior to this; and a civilization based on such a recapitulation of the past within the individual and of the individual within the past would give rise to a general resurgence of culture far exceeding that of the Renaissance. . . .

The Renaissance was the inevitable outcome of Catholicism because Catholicism, like psychoanalysis although much less so, produced a comprehensive return of the repressed. Psychoanalysis, in doing what Catholicism did, but in doing it so much more completely and effectively, will, if these speculations are correct, produce a general renaissance of culture which will go as far beyond that of the sixteenth and seventeenth centuries as psychoanalysis goes beyond Catholicism in the extent of the return of the repressed to which it will give rise. Given the current decadent state of world culture, this cannot happen too soon.

II:7

Another British sociologist, Robert Bocock, looks at similar issues. He is author of a book on Freud in the 'Key Sociologists' series (published by Ellis Horwood Ltd, Chichester and Tavistock Publications, London). The inclusion of Freud amongst the ranks of sociologists reflects the impact of his ideas on more than individual psychology. Given the need to create a bridge between those who exclusively use either sociological or psychological theories in their reflections upon pastoral care, this example of the interpenetration of the two disciples is important.

It may be difficult to 'swallow' (a good Freudian oral metaphor!) the concept of primal murder which lies at the centre of Bocock's argument (and Badcock's as well – see II:6), and to which the author refers in the first paragraph of this extract. It is essential to bear in mind that he qualifies the concept as referring to the unconscious, and not necessarily to actual history. The concept of primal murder was taken by Freud from Darwin's idea of the primal horde, where a violent and jealous father who keeps all the females to himself and drives away his sons, is then killed by the sons who devour the body of the father. In whatever terms they express it, Bocock and Badcock both address problems of living in modern Western society since the decline of the influence of religion.

Religion and the Primal Father [4]

The unconscious is timeless – so although in one sense the primal murder took place a very long time ago, in the more fundamental sense it takes place always. Every baby has murderous impulses towards its symbolic father. These wishes are so powerful for children, neurotics and for primitives (that is those whose uncon-

4. From R. J. Bocock, 'The Symbolism of the Father – a Freudian Sociological Analysis' (*The British Journal of Sociology*, June 1979, vol. 30: no. 2, pp. 206–17).

scious processes dominate them in any era), that their impact on the child, neurotic or primitive is as strong as if they had actually murdered the father. So Freud insists on saying that the primal murder was not just a wish, but an actual event, so that the impact on the modern reader is sufficiently strong. . . .

It is a postulate of psychoanalysis that religion is to be understood on the pattern of individual neurotic symptoms. Religions are not caused by individual neurosis, but religion is best understood as if it were a symptom of a neurosis of humanity as a whole.

In *The Future of an Illusion* Freud picks up a point he had made in his 1907 paper 'Obsessive Acts and Religious Practices',[5] viz. religious rituals provide the believer with a social, collective, method of handling the problems which would otherwise necessitate a private neurosis. That is, neurotic symptoms, for psychoanalysis, are produced by polymorphously perverse sexual impulses,[6] which cannot find any outlet because of the internalized cultural values. The superego can be so severe in some people that they cannot even acknowledge these impulses, and certainly cannot act upon them in perverse actions. Neurotic symptoms are substitutes for these forbidden actions. Religions can provide some substitute gratifications which are socially allowed and performed. Participants in religious rituals may be spared having to construct their own private neurosis, which might otherwise isolate them from others, and make them grow more ill over time as a consequence of this isolation. Freud does not specify what these may be in any detail. Some have been mentioned, concerned with human sacrifice and sensual rituals. Holy communion is a sublimated form of cannibalism for the believer in transubstantiation. Homosexual impulses may be satisfied for some men in their brotherly love for Jesus and other Christians. Women can enjoy a sublimated form of love for a young man in the form of Jesus, and his representative, the priest. Oedipal wishes are handled not just in terms of a killing of a god, a representative of the father, but also in prayer for protection and love from God the father, and devotions to the Blessed Virgin Mary. For men, this is a powerful form of sublimated desire for their mother. Such are some of the socially provided substitute gratifications in religion. (The arts may also provide similar substitute gratifications for some people.)

However, this does not mean that religion is positive in all its effects. It is based on illusions, that is on unconscious wishes.

5. See II:4.
6. A technical Freudian term describing various expressions of sexuality, in childhood and in adult-life – Ed.

30

Illusions do not necessarily contradict reality. Later, Freud saw religion as based on delusions – that is wishes which do contradict reality. Belief in life after death, or reincarnation, can be seen as beliefs based on wishes – most people do not know any rational arguments for them. They can be seen as either illusions or delusions; it is a matter of judgement. . . .

The prime task of psychoanalytic therapy is to aim to reduce the demands of a severe superego on the individual neurotic (i.e. the demands of the internalized primal father).

There is a basic layer of guilt in everyone, however, which fuels the superego's demands, for by conforming the person hopes to make reparation. Reparation to both the primal father, for he still persists in the archaic component of the unconscious, and to the person's own father, for he is hated as a representative of the primal father's demands for renunciation of instinctual pleasure, and as erotic rival. The symbol of the father in the unconscious is fundamental and is therefore the key link between the phylogenetic and the ontogenetic[7] levels of analysis.

The social institutions of religion, law, and politics represent the cultural superego in the demands they make. They perpetuate the primal guilt by their high demands which ordinary people cannot meet. The destructive aggressivity of the death instincts is turned on to the members of the group or the followers of the movement by this manufacture of guilt. The danger, in Freud's view, was that the amount of instinctual renunciation being demanded was too great. It led to discontents and to neuroses. It might also lead to the band of brothers, which can be read as including sisters, being formed to seek to kill the hated primal father again.

It can be argued that at least the rituals of Christianity provided a way in which this could be done without people having to be killed. These religious methods are finished for many people today – so the alternatives of art and politics have to be used. Art can appeal to a few, but may not be enough compensation for the renunciation of the desire to kill the father again. Politics offers more direct satisfaction in the manoeuvrings and word fights which normally go on in political group meetings. The danger of the re-enactment of the primal parricide is however, always present. The artistic and religious substitutes may not prove enough, and the instinctual gratifications of normal politics may prove too weak for many, so that more action is demanded. The historical situ-

7. 'Phylogenetic' refers to the birth and development of the human race; 'ontogenetic' to the birth and development of the individual. – Ed.

ation can then be awaited, or manufactured, in which the primal crime can be performed.

II:8

Confirmation of the neuroticism present in the working out of an individual's faith also comes from within the pastoral tradition. Leslie Weatherhead, one of the first British pastors to take Freud's work seriously, outlines ways in which religion can be distorted and misused. His 'Psychology, Religion and Healing' (first published in 1951) represents a good example of discriminating use of the psychological challenge, at the same time reinforcing all that is positive in religious belief and experience. A similarly positive approach to integration of psychoanalysis and religion is found in R. S. Lee's 'Freud and Christianity' (Harmondsworth, Penguin Books, 1967).

The Misuse of Christian Experience [8]

The strength of the case of the critic who calls Christian experience neurotic lies in the fact that so few Christian people advertise in their experience what true Christianity is. So far from it being 'dope', or 'illusion', or 'escapism', or 'wishful thinking', it is so spartan and costly in its demands that man turns away from them to easier ways of living, retaining its comforting aspect, but refusing its challenge, and thus giving the critic the kind of evidence he seeks. The authentic Christian experience is a courageous trafficking with reality, so demanding that it may take from man all that he has, drive him out of all his human securities, separate him from his dearest friends and ask of him life itself. I have personally known, in other lands, Christians who have paid a terrible price for their faith, and who have told me how infinitely worth while it was. Their species of Christian experience one might call the real, unadulterated article. It is a sublime thing to witness, and its effect on others has been incalculable. Here, one feels, is the strongest evidence for the authenticity and validity of Christian experience.

Few, however, show forth to the world an undistorted Christian

8. From L. D. Weatherhead, *Psychology, Religion and Healing* (London, Hodder and Stoughton, rev. edn 1955), pp. 418–24. See also VI:30 and VI:34 for similar analysis of narcissism, but applied to pastoral counselling.

experience, and, seeing the distortion caused by our neurotic trends, the critic labels the experience itself neurotic.

It seems to me important to notice some of the more common ways in which Christian experience is distorted by neurosis.

1. *Christian experience is misused to cover a flight from reality.*
Freud would have plenty of material for his thesis that religion is a projection of the father-complex if he did the work of a Christian minister for six months. People who have been criticised by others, even justly and truly, pour out to God their hurt feelings in the spirit of a child whose attitude could be described thus: 'My critics are "horrid" to me, but I know You, my Heavenly Father, will be kind to me and comfort me.' Their time of prayer and quiet becomes a neurotic orgy of self-pity in which the 'self' is projected on to God, a father substitute, who, to their neurotic imagination, must always offer them the candy and cushions of comfort. Unfortunately, the Bible can be quoted only too readily to support this distorted view. . . .

2. *Christian experience is misused to provide a false security.*
All the way through life man searches for security. The child looks for it in the love and protection of his parents, the adolescent in friends and, perhaps, the schoolmasters and schoolmistresses most admired, the lover in the beloved, the artist and poet and musician in beauty, and so on. For ever we search for that which 'will not let us down', for an abiding reality in which the soul may rest.

All this is right and, indeed, inevitable, but the truly religious man knows that ultimately there is only one final security, and that is the love of God as it is revealed in Christ. All else can be taken from us, but this, the Christian believes, will never fail.

Yet, again and again, true Christianity is distorted by men's fears. Physical safety is still held to be the reward of the righteous. . . . All this is neurotic nonsense; the distortion of true religion by the patient's neurotic trends. Christ Himself promised His followers persecution and death, and after a life of flawless loveliness spent in healing and teaching, God did not send one angel, or lift one finger, to save Him from the torture and death meted out by Rome to the vilest criminals. One would have thought that such an end would have destroyed such a heresy. But the neurotic is typically swayed by emotion, not reason, and because he has predetermined what he would like religion to be – an insurance against calamity . . .

3. *Christian experience is misused in a deceptive attempt to buy escape from the results of sin.*

Here again I must summarize an important position. The death of Christ is said to accomplish man's salvation, and this idea is twisted by the neurotic to mean that because Jesus died on the Cross, man will be 'let off' the results of his sin. . . .

For clarity's sake I repeat here some points already made in the chapter on Guilt. It is better to separate the ideas of penalty from those of consequence. The chief *penalties* of sin are separation from God and the deterioration of the sinner's character. Real Christian experience clearly ends penalty. There is penitence for the past, a new beginning, and a new orientation and direction of life. The process of integration through religion begins. . . .

What *is* neurotic is the absurdity of the idea of laying guilt on Him and expecting to be 'let off' the consequences of sin, while one is in a universe where every cause has its effect. . . .

Few things are more needed in the modern Church than teaching which exposes the neurotic and false interpretation of Christ's death, which sings hymns about being washed in His blood, as though His death were the expiation of the wrath of an angry God at a time when His beloved Son was perfectly doing His Father's will; as though, by an act of credulous superstition called 'believing faith' a sinner could break the chain of cause and effect, lay his dirty sins on the innocent Son of god, and escape consequences which are inescapably registered in the molecules of his body and the fibres of his brain.

4. *Christian experience is further misused in the interests of the superego to produce a 'holiness' that is self-centred and narcissistic.* . . .

A Christianity which, even in quest of holiness, makes a man think only of his own perfection, love only himself, and 'saving his own soul' is a Christianity distorted by neurotic trends. It loses that missionary fervour which in the first century was its most characteristic note. 'He that loveth his own soul, loseth it.'

Christianity should be studied as it was proclaimed in the open air of Galilee by Jesus Christ Himself. We should not judge it after it has been twisted by sectarian theologians who have sometimes prostituted it to satisfy their own preconceived opinions. The charge that Christianity is itself a neurosis could never have been levelled if men had proclaimed it and lived it as Christ did. It is not Christianity that is neurotic, but spurious imitations falsely called by its name. No great leader has proved less neurotic. . . .

Religious experience should be a progressive and patient

34

attempt to understand with the mind God's purposes, to respond with the feelings to His love by loving others, and to fulfil with the will, as far as we can, His purposes. If religious experience is less than this; if it becomes dope, or an insurance, or an escape, or a flight from reality, or an attempt to buy favour and escape consequences, then it is not the Christian religion, and not any religion worth having. In such cases it is so poisoned by neurotic factors as to be worse than useless. Since, in so many places, it is so poisoned, it is not surprising that many psychologists look askance at their patient's 'faith' and feel that his 'religion' is maintaining his neurotic condition. In such a situation a psychotherapist may feel it his duty to discourage his patient from religious practices until he can view the matter more normally, see things in a right perspective and rid his 'religion' of its neurotic distortion.

II:9

In 'The Christian Neurosis' *the French psychiatrist Pierre Solignac gives many examples of patients he has seen, whose emotional disability and fragility has been fuelled by their upbringing in and membership of the Catholic Church. Rather than include what becomes in the end a somewhat tedious catalogue of disasters, I include his final plea, in which he summarizes the need for a neurotic Church to die to itself, and the necessity of a new style of Christian education. It is worth comparing his picture of Catholicism, as experienced from within, with the more idealized picture of Catholicism in Badcock (see II:6) and the plea in each for a new system of education – in Badcock's case one that is based upon the insights of psychoanalysis.*

The Revolution Never Born [9]

Christian education is in perpetual conflict with the message of the gospel, and it is based on a serious contradiction.

At a very early stage the child to whom one speaks of love and giving himself is subjected to a series of prohibitions and taboos, and told that if he goes wrong he puts himself in a state of sin. He is prevented from discovering pleasure and joy. All pleasure

9. From P. Solignac, *The Christian Neurosis* (London, SCM Press, 1982), pp. 163–6.

is sin. Sexual pleasure is clearly the prime sin, all the more in that educators, priests, religious, old women or good traditionalist Christians are deprived of it. Some project their obsessive frustration on the children whom they bring up or, more precisely, whom they make to feel guilty.

Freud defined libido as the energy derived from sexual drives. In Jung, the notion of libido is expanded to the point of denoting the 'psychical energy' generally present in everything that is a 'tendency towards'. In denying the importance of the sexual drive, its development and its realization, Christian education creates an inhibition of psychological energy, mental tone and the pleasure of living in general.

Think of the number of castrated Christians which this has produced, who, caught between desire and defence, live in fear of everything! Phobic, anxious, sometimes physically ill or impotent, they lead their petty lives, psychologically cramped, day to day in all good conscience constructing their eternal salvation. . . .

The Christian must identify himself with Jesus Christ, who was the very type of the free man, challenging all the structures of his time. In fact, Jesus relativized the law. His teaching brought about a profound change in relations between people and the institution constructed by this law and charged with its observance: he redefined the way which leads to God, the love of one's neighbour and not legalism. He shifted the centre of gravity in religion and rendered useless any institution organized for the defence and maintenance of the law. That was the real cause of his execution. . . .

Jesus always struggled against rites and against the neurotic observance of the law. He denounced legal stupidity and niggardliness: when people censured him for having cured on the sabbath day, he replied: 'Which of you, if he has a sheep fallen into a pit on the sabbath day, will not go to get it out?' His whole attitude was based on a single law: his effective love of his neighbour. He does not constrict himself by adding up transgressions of the law. For him the faith of the paralysed man or the love of the sinful woman proves that they are near to God: they have understood the meaning of 'the kingdom of God'. . . .

Jesus did not follow the way of John the Baptist. He did not retire into the desert to live a life of fasting and asceticism. He stayed among people, making contact with all social classes, both the religious professionals and those of doubtful morality. He did not think it beneath him to join in a wedding or to drink wine. He lived with a freedom which no god-fearing man dared allow. His attitude threatened the social and religious equilibrium of the

Judaism of the first century. His authority and his liberty explain conflicts which, provoked by what he said, finally led to his condemnation.

His message was that of the anti-neurotic: faced with a rigid society, legalistic and mistrusting, he showed that only communication, love and respect for people, no matter whom, led to God. His message was not that of fear, anxiety or guilt. It was that of a free man, accepting no compromise and preferring to transgress rather than to obey a coercive and infantilizing law. It is incomprehensible that such a message could have given birth to a neurotic church with an attitude of perpetual compromise.

People have said that Christianity was a revolution which was never born. The church always has been and remains the institution most capable of thwarting all revolutions. It has been rapidly integrated into patrimonial society, based on the family, property and inheritance. It became a hierarchical institution, with its own structures and its temporal interests to defend. Even worse, however, it completely changed the meaning of its initial message. It established a morality founded not on love but on fear of death and the last judgement. It based its education on the crucifixion and not on the resurrection: Christ was crucified because of his love and his liberal behaviour, all qualities which do not accord well with the needs of a church and an organization. But he was raised and by the same token acknowledged to be Son of God.

Crucifixion and resurrection: the real problem lies there. The death to self favoured by Christian morality is not submission to the other person; it is not submission to a legalistic superego inculcating feelings of guilt. Its meaning is quite different: to die to oneself is to lose the primitive narcissism which makes someone incapable of any real social life and any deep relationship with others. It is to pass from being an object, subject to prohibitions and taboos, to being a responsible, autonomous subject, capable of loving oneself and others deeply. There, it seems to me, is the real sense of resurrection which makes us free men, sons of God.

Part III

The Validation of Religion and Faith

III:10

It is one thing to use the psychological critique to prune religion of its diseased wood and render it less harmful. It is another to stake out, again from a psychological position, the positive value of, or even necessity for, healthy religion as an essential part of the wholeness of the individual. Some psychologists, although critical of the faults of institutionalized religion, have underlined the importance of faith. Many of them have come from the Freudian stable, but for one reason or another have broken away from the strict Freudian line. Perhaps because they have in common the experience of being treated as heretics by a monolithic Freudian movement, they are able to identify with the fate of those who have similarly suffered in the history of the Church in debates about orthodoxy, and tend to support the individual who has been able to break free from the bonds of an authoritarian church.

Jung was one of the first to leave the Freudian charmed circle, partly because of conscious and unconscious motives on the part of both him and Freud, but also because of a profound disagreement between them over the more positive aspects of religion. Is it because Jung is seen as one of the first to stand up to Freud that he has been espoused by Christians, who do not on the whole know how to deal with the analysis of their faith made by 'the godless Jew'? (see II:5) Yet Jung was scarcely a conventional Christian in his beliefs or in his life. It is always a temptation, in pursuit of confirmation of one's own beliefs or prejudices (see VI:33), to lift phrases out of context, and this is especially easy with the work of such productive writers as Freud or Jung.

Jung is for the most part a more difficult author to understand than Freud. At times the poetry and mysticism of his writing gives prominence to a sense of the numinous which for some may be a welcome counterweight to Freud's reductionist materialism. His use of parallels from many different cultures is impressive on an intellectual level because it demonstrates his wide knowledge; and is satisfying on an emotional level for the person who wants to make all things into a whole. Yet it needs to be said that in terms

38

of analytic practice Jungians in Britain are much closer today to the other analytic schools than a cursory reading of Jung and Freud might suggest. This may mean that in the actual practice of pastoral care and counselling the division is not as significant as it might seem to some Christian apologists. Nevertheless, in the interests of the Jungian emphasis on the creative tension between opposites, and from one of his more readily understood works, let Jung speak for himself:

Psychotherapists or the Clergy? [1]

There are many well-educated patients who flatly refuse to consult the clergyman. With the philosopher they will have even less to do, for the history of philosophy leaves them cold, and intellectual problems seem to them more barren than the desert. And where are the great and wise men who do not merely talk about the meaning of life and of the world, but really possess it? Human thought cannot conceive any system or final truth that could give the patient what he needs in order to live: that is, faith, hope, love and insight.

These four highest achievements of human effort are so many gifts of grace, which are neither to be taught nor learned, neither given nor taken, neither withheld nor earned, since they come through experience, which is something *given*, and therefore beyond the reach of human caprice. Experiences cannot be *made*. They happen – yet fortunately their independence of man's activity is not absolute but relative. We can draw closer to them – that much lies within our human reach. . . .

Thus, in trying to meet the demands made upon him, the doctor is confronted by a question which seems to contain an insuperable difficulty. How can he help the sufferer to attain the liberating experience which will bestow upon him the four great gifts of grace and heal his sickness? We can of course advise the patient with the very best intentions that he should have true love, or true faith, or true hope; and we can admonish him with the phrase: 'Know thyself'. But how is the patient, before he has come to experience, to obtain that which only experience can give him? . . .

We have come to a serious pass. The exodus from the German Protestant Church is only one of many symptoms which should

1. From C. G. Jung, 'Psychotherapists or the Clergy' in *Modern Man in Search of a Soul* (London, Routledge and Kegan Paul, 1961), pp. 260–7, 277–82.

make it plain to the clergy that mere admonitions to believe, or to perform acts of charity, do not give modern man what he is looking for. The fact that many clergymen seek support or practical help from Freud's theory of sexuality or Adler's theory of power is astonishing, inasmuch as both these theories are hostile to spiritual values, being, as I have said, psychology without the psyche. They are rational methods of treatment which actually hinder the realization of meaningful experience. By far the larger number of psychotherapists are disciples of Freud or of Adler. This means that the great majority of patients are necessarily alienated from a spiritual standpoint – a fact which cannot be a matter of indifference to one who has the realization of spiritual values much at heart. The wave of interest in psychology which at present is sweeping over the Protestant countries of Europe is far from receding. It is coincident with the general exodus from the Church. . . .

I should like to call attention to the following facts. During the past thirty years, people from all the civilized countries of the earth have consulted me. I have treated many hundreds of patients, the larger number being Protestants, a smaller number Jews, and not more than five or six believing Catholics. Among all my patients in the second half of life – that is to say, over thirty-five – there has not been one whose problem in the last resort was not that of finding a religious outlook on life. It is safe to say that every one of them fell ill because he had lost that which the living religions of every age have given to their followers, and none of them has been really healed who did not regain his religious outlook. This of course has nothing whatever to do with a particular creed or membership of a church. . . .

It seems to me, that, side by side with the decline of religious life, the neuroses grow noticeably more frequent. There are as yet no statistics which enable us to prove this increase in actual numbers. But of one thing I am sure, that everywhere the mental state of European man shows an alarming lack of balance. We are living undeniably in a period of the greatest restlessness, nervous tension, confusion and disorientation of outlook. Among my patients from many countries, all of them educated persons, there is a considerable number who came to see me, not because they were suffering from a neurosis, but because they could find no meaning in life or were torturing themselves with questions which neither present-day philosophy nor religion could answer. Some of them perhaps thought that I knew of a magic formula, but I was soon forced to tell them that I, too, had no answer to give. And this brings us to practical considerations.

40

Let us take for example that most ordinary and frequent of questions: What is the meaning of my life, or of life in general? . . . It must be a relief to every serious-minded person to hear that the psychotherapist also does not know what to say. Such a confession is often the beginning of the patient's confidence in him. . . .

The psychotherapist who takes his work seriously must come to grips with this question. He must decide in every single case whether or not he is willing to stand by a human being with counsel and help upon what may be a daring misadventure. He must have no fixed ideas as to what is right, nor must he pretend to know what is right and what not – otherwise he takes something from the richness of the experience. He must keep in view what actually happens – and only that which acts, is actual. If something which seems to me an error shows itself to be more effective than a truth, then I must first follow up the error, for in it lie power and life which I lose if I hold to what seems to me true. Light has need of darkness – otherwise how could it appear as light?

It is well known that Freudian psychoanalysis is limited to the task of making conscious the shadow-side and the evil within us. It simply brings into action the civil war that was latent, and lets it go at that. The patient must deal with it as best he can. Freud has unfortunately overlooked the fact that man has never yet been able singlehanded to hold his own against the powers of darkness – that is, of the unconscious. Man has always stood in need of the spiritual help which each individual's own religion held out to him. The opening up of the unconscious always means the outbreak of intense spiritual suffering; it is as when a flourishing civilization is abandoned to invading hordes of barbarians, or when fertile fields are exposed by the bursting of a dam to a raging torrent. . . . Man has been aware of this danger since the earliest times, even in the most primitive stages of culture. It was to arm himself against this threat and to heal the damage done, that he developed religious and magical practices. This is why the medicine-man is also the priest; he is the saviour of the body as well as of the soul, and religions are systems of healing for psychic illness. This is especially true of the two greatest religions of man, Christianity and Buddhism. Man is never helped in his suffering by what he thinks for himself, but only by revelations of a wisdom greater than his own. It is this which lifts him out of his distress.

Today this eruption of destructive forces has already taken place, and man suffers from it in spirit. That is why patients force the psychotherapist into the rôle of a priest, and expect and demand of him that he shall free them from their distress. That

41

is why we psychotherapists must occupy ourselves with problems which, strictly speaking, belong to the theologian. But we cannot leave these questions for theology to answer; the urgent, psychic needs of suffering people confront us with them day after day. Since, as a rule, every concept and viewpoint handed down from the past fails us, we must first tread with the patient the path of his illness – the path of his mistake that sharpens his conflicts and increases his loneliness till it grows unbearable – hoping that from the psychic depths which cast up the powers of destruction the rescuing forces will come also. . . .

It is as though, at the culmination of the illness, the destructive powers were converted into healing forces. This is brought about by the fact that the archetypes come to independent life and serve as spiritual guides for the personality, thus supplanting the inadequate ego with its futile willing and striving. As the religious-minded person would say: guidance has come from God. With most of my patients I have to avoid this formulation, for it reminds them too much of what they have to reject. I must express myself in more modest terms, and say that the psyche has awakened to spontaneous life. . . . To the patient it is nothing less than a revelation when, from the hidden depths of the psyche, something arises to confront him – something strange that is not the 'I' and is therefore beyond the reach of personal caprice. He has gained access to the sources of psychic life, and this marks the beginning of the cure. . . .

The living spirit grows and even outgrows its earlier forms of expression; it freely chooses the men in whom it lives and who proclaim it. This living spirit is eternally renewed and pursues its goal in manifold and inconceivable ways throughout the history of mankind. Measured against it, the names and forms which men have given it mean little enough; they are only the changing leaves and blossoms on the stem of the eternal tree.

III:11

Like all therapies, the Jungian has its technical terms: for example, 'archetypes' (upon which whole books have been written); or, more simple to understand, 'the shadow' (the dark side) and 'anima/ animus' (the unconscious feminine/masculine counterpart to male or female consciousness). Since religious faith is also full of symbols, the dialogue between Jungian theory and religion seems an obvious one. James Hillman explores, in this extract, the significance of the feminine principle (anima) for religion and wholeness.

It is important to notice the totally distinct interpretation of incest-uous phantasies which the Jungian makes, although the treatment of symbolism as representative of aspects of the total self bears a close resemblance to object-relations theory, which has come to occupy a significant place in British post-Freudian theory and prac-tice. This resemblance is one reason for the closer working relation-ship beginning to take place between the different psychodynamic schools in Britain, referred to above.

The importance of the feminine here is totally different from, for example, Dyson's reference to the importance of feminist theology in VI:35; and although it helps the feminine to be acknowledged in this collection of readings, it has to be said that pastoral coun-selling, and for the most part pastoral care, remains male-domi-nated, at least in its literature, unlike Freudian, Kleinian and Jungian psychotherapies, which have received major insights from women analysts and writers. The general lack of women writers in pastoral care and counselling must therefore be a reflection of the status of women generally in the Church.

The Religious Moment [2]

As consciousness moves away from identification with the mind and ego, becoming broader and more feminine in its receptivity and self-intimacy, the flesh as well transforms into body consciousness. . . . Body consciousness begins with the inner experience of the flesh, the actual incarnation of our humanity in warmth and joy and ease and rhythm and being present here and now, physically close to ourselves, to our symptoms and sensations, and to the physical reality of others. . . .

This way to the body is through the unconscious rather than through the conscious mind, which too often tends to stand apart from it, regarding it as an object, albeit a precious one – yes, even 'mine', but unfortunately not the real 'me', somehow still an 'it'. Then the flesh and its life become more compelling, so that the more we are cut off from it, the more it fascinates us, autoerot-ically to draw our attention back into it. The natural anima, that tawny-skinned swimmer, the playful and cat-like one, and the moods and fantasies she construes, lead one downward into animal warmth, physical moods and sensations. The cramped symptoms, the worry over the flesh as object and what can go wrong with 'it', at last have a chance to fall away.

2. From J. Hillman, *Insearch: Psychology and Religion* (New York, Charles Scrib-ner's Sons, 1967), pp. 122–6.

The longing to become whole again, healed in flesh and resurrected into body, does not have to be achieved through an outer forbidden sexual union, even though this is frequently the way a man feels he can be redeemed, his body given back to him again. In fact, the deepest intimacy with his own physical feelings is expressed in the psyche of a man by the image of the 'sister' with whom an outer sexual union is forbidden. Yet as accompaniment to these crucial emotions the psyche insists upon the sister-image. Behind the attraction to the forbidden woman is the fascination of the 'sister'. To take her only reductively as infantile incestuous desires distorts her deepest meaning. . . . My sister has my father and my mother, and my upbringing. We share the same secrets. She is of my blood and bone. My sister is me – but feminine. To unite with her is to enter myself, fertilize myself, for 'incest is union of like with like'. . . . She awakens the original image of wholeness before the early wounds of childhood split good from bad, ego from Self, body from flesh, male from female. Through her I can be reconciled in love to my own physical nature. . . .

Befriending the body is the fundamental yea-saying to physical life as a temple or vessel of something trans-physical. And this intimacy and familiarity with the body by creeping down into it and listening to it from within is the necessary counter-pole to activation of the unconscious in phantasy and dream. Without the two together, and together always, we easily slide into the old Kantian mistake of overvaluing mental contents, taking them as the only expression of the psyche which in idealist philosophy cannot be touched. Whenever the physical is devalued, something is being done against the feminine side. Incarnation, psychologically witnessed, is the feeling of life in the flesh. Resurrection of this flesh, from a psychological view, refers to the transformation of flesh into body, parallel to the transformation of egotistic will and rationality into psychic consciousness. This transformation refers also to the maturing of the body within the aging flesh. Even while submitting to the irreversible process of aging, one moves forward with the changes of maturing. Despite the ugliness of aging one feels more grateful and becomes more graceful, that is, 'full of grace', which also means that the body is the place of grace. Again, grace is a feminine virtue and again the descent of this grace depends upon the prior descent into the feminity of flesh and its redemption as body.

I do not believe that the religious moment is something altogether different from what we have been unfolding in this chapter. . . .

The personality that cannot contain itself, that falls into bits

44

should the ego be abandoned, that has no other light but that held together by the will, is hardly the ground for a religious moment. Even if God be love, that love can shatter us if our wounds from early human loves are fragilely stitched together. Can the personality that has not taken into account in one way or another the unconscious, the shadow and the anima, be a vessel to hold a divine force? . . .

The religious moment as described in traditional accounts is a vivid intense realization, transcending ego and revealing truth. Just this is also at what analysis aims. The truth which can be experienced there goes beyond the causal truth of oneself: the banalities of how I got this way and who is to blame and what must I do now. Analysis moves toward the larger truth of coherence, toward intimations of immortality, how my person fits into the larger scheme of fate. These revelations, by opening one door to my emotional center, illumine one corner of the darkness. This truth is also love since it gives the sense of belonging and attachment to one's own ground.

If the main shadow of counseling is love and if counseling lies in its shadow, then our work will depend on love's 'perfection'. Love, as *agape*, means 'to receive', 'to welcome', 'to embrace'. Perhaps the perfection of love begins through faith in and work on the feminine within us, man or woman, since the feminine ground is the embracing container, receiving, holding, and carrying. It gives birth and nourishes and it encourages us to believe. This ground welcomes us home to ourselves just as we are. I do not know how better or how else we can prepare for the religious moment than by cultivating, giving inner culture to, our own unconscious feminity. For the religious moment to touch us at least the ground can be worked and opened, within the range of our individual human limits.

[*There is a considerable amount of literature which relates Jungian thinking to Christian faith and practice. Space forbids the inclusion of further readings on this aspect, although the work of Christopher Bryant must be mentioned.*[3]]

3. e.g. C. Bryant, *The Heart in Pilgrimage* (London, Darton Longman and Todd, 1980); C. Bryant, *Jung and the Christian Way* (London, Darton Longman and Todd, 1983). See also: W. Clift, *Jung and Christianity* (Crossroad Pub./SPCK, 1982).

It is important to recognize that it is not only Jungian writers who have been sympathetic to the relevance of faith. Four readings now demonstrate the significance of religion in other psychologists – Fromm, Erikson, Maslow and Allport. Although Carl Rogers has been a major influence on counselling technique, his writing does not yield anything of particular value to the theme of this reader – indeed, the potentially most interesting, a transcript of a conversation with Martin Buber, leaves Rogers in the shade! Although his impact on counselling generally has been immense (and in some quarters he appears to be as idealized as much as Freud or Jung are in others), in British pastoral counselling he is probably less influential than the psychodynamic schools.

Erich Fromm was a neo-Freudian. Invited like many other Berlin analysts to emigrate to the United States during the thirties, he recognized, as many others then did, the importance of cultural factors in human development. Like most neo-Freudians, he was interested not only in the individual and the immediate family, but also in the influence of society, history and culture. Fromm's interests have ranged wide, and his clear style and significant themes have made his books deservedly popular (e.g. 'The Art of Loving', 'Fear of Freedom', 'Man for Himself', *etc.). His* 'Dogma of Christ' *(London, Routledge and Kegan Paul, 1963) contains what I can only clumsily call a psycho-socio-historical view of the christological debates in the early Church, as well as other essays. If Fromm's concerns on an existential level bear closely upon matters of faith and living, it is perhaps no surprise to learn that he was one of a circle of friends which included such key figures as Paul Tillich (see V: 27), Abraham Maslow (see III:14), Karen Horney and the Zen analyst, Suzuki.*

Authoritarian and Humanistic Religion [4]

I want to make it clear at the outset that I understand by religion *any system of thought and action shared by a group which gives the individual a frame of orientation and an object of devotion.*

There is indeed no culture of the past, and it seems there can be no culture in the future, which does not have religion in this broad sense of our definition. We need not, however, stop at this

---

4. From E. Fromm, *Psychoanalysis and Religion* (Yale Univ. Press, and New York, Bantam Books, 1967), pp. 21–6, 32–8, 49–51.

merely descriptive statement. The study of man permits us to recognize that the need for a common system of orientation and for an object of devotion is deeply rooted in the conditions of human existence. I have attempted in *Man for Himself* to analyze the nature of this need, and I quote from that book:

Self-awareness, reason, and imagination have disrupted the 'harmony' which characterizes animal existence. Their emergence has made man into an anomaly, into the freak of the universe. He is part of nature, subject to her physical laws and unable to change them, yet he transcends the rest of nature. He is set apart while being a part; he is homeless, yet chained to the home he shares with all creatures. Cast into this world at an accidental place and time, he is forced out of it, again accidentally. Being aware of himself, he realizes his powerlessness and the limitations of his existence. He visualizes his own end: death. Never is he free from the dichotomy of his existence: he cannot rid himself of his mind, even if he should want to; he cannot rid himself of his body as long as he is alive – and his body makes him want to be alive.

Reason, man's blessing, is also his curse; it forces him to cope everlastingly with the task of solving an insoluble dichotomy. Human existence is different in this respect from that of all other organisms; it is in a state of constant and unavoidable disequilibrium. Man's life cannot 'be lived' by repeating the pattern of his species; *he* must live. Man is the only animal that can be *bored*, that can be *discontented*, that can feel evicted from paradise. Man is the only animal for whom his own existence is a problem which he has to solve and from which he cannot escape. He cannot go back to the prehuman state of harmony with nature; he must proceed to develop his reason until he becomes the master of nature, and of himself. . . .

Having lost paradise, the unity with nature, he has become the eternal wanderer (Odysseus, Oedipus, Abraham, Faust); he is impelled to go forward and with everlasting effort to make the unknown known by filling in with answers the blank spaces of his knowledge. He must give account to himself of himself, and of the meaning of his existence. He is driven to overcome this inner split, tormented by a craving for 'absoluteness,' for another kind of harmony which can lift the curse by which he was separated from nature, from his fellow men, and from himself.

There is no one without a religious need, a need to have a frame of orientation and an object of devotion; but this statement does not tell us anything about a specific context in which this religious need is manifest. Man may worship animals, trees, idols of gold or stone, an invisible god, a saintly man or diabolic leaders; he may worship his ancestors, his nation, his class or party, money or success; his religion may be conducive to the development of destructiveness or of love, of domination or of brotherliness; it may further his power of reason or paralyze it; he may be aware of his system as being a religious one, different from those of the secular realm, or he may think that he has no religion and interpret his devotion to certain allegedly secular aims like power, money or success as nothing but his concern for the practical and expedient. The question is not *religion or not* but *which kind of religion*, whether it is one furthering man's development, the unfolding of his specifically human powers, or one paralyzing them.

[*Fromm then restates Freud's connection between neurosis and religion (see II:4) but emphasizes more strongly that neurosis can be a private form of religion. He gives some examples of private religion, and then goes on*:]

There is one important difference between a religious cult and neurosis which makes the cult vastly superior to the neurosis as far as the satisfaction gained is concerned. If we imagine that the patient with his neurotic fixation to his father lived in a culture where ancestor worship is generally practiced as a cult, he could share his feelings with his fellow men rather than feel himself isolated. And it is the feeling of isolation, of being shut-out, which is the painful sting of every neurosis. Even the most irrational orientation if it is shared by a considerable body of men gives the individual the feeling of oneness with others, a certain amount of security and stability which the neurotic person lacks. There is nothing inhuman, evil, or irrational which does not give some comfort provided it is shared by a group. The most convincing proof for this statement can be found in those incidents of mass madness of which we have been and still are witnesses. Once a doctrine, however irrational, has gained power in a society, millions of people will believe in it rather than feel ostracized and isolated.

These ideas lead to an important consideration concerning the function of religion. If man regresses so easily into a more primitive form of religion, have not the monotheistic religions today the function of saving man from such regression? Is not the belief in God a safeguard against falling back into ancestor, totem, or golden-calf worship? Indeed, this would be so if religion had succeeded in molding man's character according to its stated ideals. But historical religion has capitulated before and compromised with secular power again and again. It has been concerned far more with certain dogmas rather than with the practice of love and humility in everyday life. . . . The question must be asked, not from an antireligious point of view but out of concern for man's soul: Can we trust religion to be the representative of religious needs or must we not separate these needs from organized, traditional religion in order to prevent the collapse of our moral structure?

In considering an answer to this question we must remember that no intelligent discussion of the problem is possible as long as we deal with religion in general instead of differentiating between various types of religion and religious experience. It would far transcend the scope of this chapter to attempt a review of all types of religion. Even to discuss only those types which are relevant from the psychological standpoint cannot be undertaken here. I shall therefore deal with only one distinction, but one which in my opinion is the most important, and which cuts across non-theistic and theistic religions; that between *authoritarian* and *humanistic* religions.

What is the principle of authoritarian religion? The definition of religion given in the *Oxford Dicionary*, while attempting to define religion as such, is a rather accurate definition of authoritarian religion. It reads: '[Religion is] recognition on the part of man of some higher unseen power as having control of his destiny, and as being entitled to obedience, reverence, and worship.'

Here the emphasis is on the recognition that man is controlled by a higher power outside of himself. But this alone does not constitute authoritarian religion. What makes it so is the idea that this power, because of the control it exercises, is *entitled* to 'obedience, reverence and worship.' I italicize the word 'entitled' because it shows that the reason for worship, obedience, and reverence lies not in the moral qualities of the deity, not in love or justice, but in the fact that it has control, that is, has power over man. Furthermore it shows that the higher power has a right to force man to worship him and that lack of reverence and obedience constitutes sin.

The essential element in authoritarian religion and in the authoritarian religious experience is the surrender to a power transcending man. The main virtue of this type of religion is obedience, its cardinal sin is disobedience. Just as the deity is conceived as omnipotent or omniscient, man is conceived as being powerless and insignificant. Only as he can gain grace or help from the deity by complete surrender can he feel strength. Submission to a powerful authority is one of the avenues by which man escapes from his feeling of aloneness and limitation. In the act of surrender he loses his independence and integrity as an individual but he gains the feeling of being protected by an awe-inspiring power of which, as it were, he becomes a part. . . .

Humanistic religion, on the contrary, is centered around man and his strength. Man must develop his power of reason in order to understand himself, his relationship to his fellow men and his position in the universe. He must recognize the truth, both with regard to his limitations and his potentialities. He must develop his powers of love for others as well as for himself and experience the solidarity of all living beings. He must have principles and norms to guide him in this aim. Religious experience in this kind of religion is the experience of oneness with the All, based on one's relatedness to the world as it is grasped with thought and with love. Man's aim in humanistic religion is to achieve the greatest strength, not the greatest powerlessness; virtue is self-realization, not obedience. Faith is certainty of conviction based on one's experience of thought and feeling, not assent to propositions on credit of the proposer. The prevailing mood is that of joy, while the prevailing mood in authoritarian religion is that of sorrow and of guilt.

Inasmuch as humanistic religions are theistic, God is a symbol of *man's own powers* which he tries to realize in his life, and is not a symbol of force and domination, having *power over man*.

Illustrations of humanistic religions are early Buddhism, Taoism, the teachings of Isaiah, Jesus, Socrates, Spinoza, certain trends in the Jewish and Christian religions (particularly mysticism), the religion of Reason of the French Revolution. It is evident from these that the distinction between authoritarian and humanistic religion cuts across the distinction between theistic and nontheistic, and between religions in the narrow sense of the word and philosophical systems of religious character. What matters in all such systems is not the thought system as such but the human attitude underlying their doctrines. . . .

While in humanistic religion God is the image of man's higher self, a symbol of what man potentially is or ought to become, in authoritarian religion God becomes the sole possessor of what was originally man's: of his reason and his love. The more perfect God becomes the more imperfect becomes man. He *projects* the best he has onto God and thus impoverishes himself. Now God has all love, all wisdom, all justice – and man is deprived of these

50

qualities, he is empty and poor. He had begun with the feeling of smallness, but he now has become completely powerless and without strength; all his powers have been projected onto God. This mechanism of projection is the very same which can be observed in interpersonal relationships of a masochistic, submissive character, where one person is awed by another and attributes his own powers and aspirations to the other person. It is the same mechanism that makes people endow the leaders of even the most inhuman systems with qualities of superwisdom and kindness.

When man has thus projected his own most valuable powers onto God, what of his relationship to his own powers? They have become separated from him and in this process he has become *alienated* from himself. Everything he has is now God's and nothing is left in him. *His only access to himself is through God.* In worshiping God he tries to get in touch with that part of himself which he has lost through projection. After having given God all he has, he begs God to return to him some of what originally was his own. But having lost his own he is completely at God's mercy. He necessarily feels like a 'sinner' since he has deprived himself of everything that is good, and it is only through God's mercy or grace that he can regain that which alone makes him human. And in order to persuade God to give him some of his love, he must prove to him how utterly deprived he is of love; in order to persuade God to guide him by his superior wisdom he must prove to him how deprived he is of wisdom when he is left to himself.

But this alienation from his own powers not only makes man feel slavishly dependent on God, it makes him bad too. He becomes a man without faith in his fellow men or in himself, without the experience of his own love, of his own power of reason. As a result the separation between the 'holy' and the 'secular' occurs. In his worldly activities man acts without love, in that sector of his life which is reserved to religion he feels himself to be a sinner (which he actually is, since to live without love is to live in sin) and tries to recover some of his lost humanity by being in touch with God. Simultaneously, he tries to win forgiveness by emphasizing his own helplessness and worthlessness. Thus the attempt to obtain forgiveness results in the activation of the very attitude from which his sins stem. He is caught in a painful dilemma. The more he praises God, the emptier he becomes. The emptier he becomes, the more sinful he feels. The more sinful he feels, the more he praises his God – and the less able is he to regain himself.

III:13

Erik Erikson cannot be classified as a strict Freudian, although he has always remained within the orthodox circle. His work on identity, particularly during its major formation in adolescence, and his model of human development, called the Eight Ages of Man (in 'Childhood and Society', Harmondsworth, Penguin, 1965), have been applied to many different aspects of pastoral care and counselling. James Fowler, for instance, is strongly influenced by Erikson in his work on the development of faith (see V:25). Erikson has also contributed to the development of psycho-history, and his major incursion into the field of religion was in his psycho-biography 'Young Man Luther'. Psychoanalysis which is not able to get confirmation from the active co-operation of a client is bound to be speculative; but at least such speculation tells us something of the author's thinking, whether or not it is valid or accurate history or biography. In the Epilogue to 'Young Man Luther' Erikson reflects for himself on the significance of faith, linking it to the first of the stages of development he has described, basic trust:

Images of Basic Trust [5]

One may say that man, when looking through a glass darkly, finds himself in an inner cosmos in which the outlines of three objects awaken dim nostalgias. One of these is the simple and fervent wish for a hallucinatory sense of unity with a maternal matrix, and a supply of benevolently powerful substances; it is symbolized by the affirmative face of charity, graciously inclined, reassuring the faithful of the unconditional acceptance of those who will return to the bosom. In this symbol the split of autonomy is for ever repaired: shame is healed by unconditional approval, doubt by the eternal presence of generous provision.

In the centre of the second nostalgia is the paternal voice of guiding conscience, which puts an end to the simple paradise of childhood and provides a sanction for energetic action. It also warns of the inevitability of guilty entanglement, and threatens with the lightning of wrath. To change the threatening sound of this voice, if need be by means of partial surrender and manifold self-castration, is the second imperative demand which enters religious endeavour. At all cost, the Godhead must be forced to

5. From E. Erikson, *Young Man Luther* (London, Faber and Faber, 1959), pp. 257–9.

indicate that He Himself mercifully planned crime and punishment in order to assure salvation.

Finally, the glass shows the pure self itself, the unborn core of creation, the – as it were, preparental – centre where God is pure nothing. . . . God is so designated in many ways in Eastern mysticism. This pure self is the self no longer sick with a conflict between right and wrong, not dependent on providers, and not dependent on guides to reason and reality.

These three images are the main religious objects. Naturally, they often fuse in a variety of ways and are joined by hosts of secondary deities. But must we call it regression if man thus seeks again the earliest encounters of his trustful past in his efforts to reach a hoped-for and eternal future? Or do religions partake of man's ability, even as he regresses, to recover creatively? At their creative best, religions retrace our earliest inner experiences, giving tangible form to vague evils, and reaching back to the earliest individual sources of trust; at the same time, they keep alive the common symbols of integrity distilled by the generations. If this is partial regression, it is a regression which, in retracing firmly established pathways, returns to the present amplified and clarified. Here, of course, much depends on whether or not the son of a given era approaches the glass in good faith: whether he seeks to find again on a higher level a treasure of basic trust safely possessed from the beginning, or tries to find a birthright denied him in the first place, in his childhood. It is clear that each generation (whatever its ideological heaven) owes to the next a safe treasure of basic trust; Luther was psychologically and ideologically right when he said in theological terms that the infant *has* faith if his community *means* his baptism. Creative moments, however, and creative periods are rare. The process here described may remain abortive or outlive itself in stagnant institutions – in which case it can and must be associated with neurosis and psychosis, with self-restriction and self-delusion, with hypocrisy and stupid moralism.

Freud has convincingly demonstrated the affinity of some religious ways of thought with those of neurosis.[6] But we regress in our dreams, too, and the inner structures of many dreams correspond to neurotic symptoms. Yet dreaming itself is a healthy activity, and a necessary one. And here too, the success of a dream depends on the faith one has, not on that which one seeks; a good conscience provides that proverbially good sleep which knits up the ravelled sleeve of care. All the things that made man

6. See II:4.

feel guilty, ashamed, doubtful, and mistrustful during the daytime are woven into a mysterious yet meaningful set of dream images, so arranged as to direct the recuperative powers of sleep toward a constructive waking state. The dreamwork fails and the dream turns into a nightmare when there is an intrusion of a sense of foreign reality into the dreamer's make-believe, and a subsequent disturbance in returning from that superimposed sense of reality into real reality.

Religions try to use mechanisms analogous to dreamlife, reinforced at times by a collective genius of poetry and artistry, to offer ceremonial dreams of great recuperative value. It is possible, however, that the medieval Church, the past master of ceremonial hallucination, by promoting the reality of hell too efficiently, and by tampering too successfully with man's sense of reality in this world, eventually created, instead of a belief in the greater reality of a more desirable world, only a sense of nightmare in this one.

I have implied that the original faith which Luther tried to restore goes back to the basic trust of early infancy. In doing so I have not, I believe, diminished the wonder of what Luther calls God's disguise. If I assume that it is the smiling face and the guiding voice of infantile parent images which religion projects on to the benevolent sky, I have no apologies to render to an age which thinks of painting the moon red. Peace comes from the inner space.

III:14

The circle of friends mentioned above – Tillich, Fromm, Maslow and others – shared a humanistic philosophy, but one which, unlike much humanism, was not against religion and one which made room for the importance of religious needs. Maslow is one of the major representatives of humanistic psychology, the third major force in psychotherapy after the psychodynamic and behaviourist schools. The fact that he attaches such significance to faith and religious- or peak-experiences, as this extract indicates, shows that in his famous 'hierarchy of needs' the term self-actualization, which is at the top of the hierarchy, is not synonymous with introverted self-sufficiency, as some people might otherwise presume.

The Validity of Religious Experience [7]

The pure, nineteenth-century scientist looks like a babbling child to sophisticated people just because he is so cocky, so self-assured, just because he doesn't know how little he knows, how limited scientific knowledge is when compared with the vast unknown.

Most powerfully is this true of the psychologist whose ratio of knowledge to mystery must be the smallest of all scientists. Indeed, sometimes I am so impressed by all that we need to know in comparison with what we do know, that I think it best to define a psychologist, not as one who knows the answers, but rather as one who struggles with the questions.

Perhaps it is because he is so innocently unaware of his smallness, of the feebleness of his knowledge, of the smallness of his playpen, or the smallness of his portion of the cosmos and because he takes his narrow limits so for granted that he reminds me of the little boy who was seen standing uncertainly at a street corner with a bundle under his arm. A concerned bypasser asked him where he was going and he replied that he was running away from home. Why was he waiting at the corner? He wasn't allowed to cross the street!

Another consequence of accepting the concept of a natural, general, basic, personal religious experience is that it will also reform atheism, agnosticism, and humanism. These doctrines have, on the whole, been simply a rejection of the churches; and they have fallen into the trap of identifying religion with the churches, a very serious mistake as we have seen. They threw out too much, as we are now discovering. The alternative that these groups have rested on has been pure science of the nineteenth-century sort, pure rationalisation insofar as they have not relied merely on negative attacks upon the organized churches. This has turned out to be not so much a solution of the problem as a retreat from it. But if it can be demonstrated that the religious questions (which were thrown out along with the churches) are valid questions, that these questions are almost the same as the deep, profound and serious ultimate concerns of the sort that Tillich talks about and of the sort by which I would define humanistic psychology, then these humanistic sects could become much more useful to mankind than they are now.

7. From A. H. Maslow, *Religious Values and Peak-Experiences* (Columbus, Ohio State Univ. Press, 1964), pp. 46–7.

III:15

Few British readers will be acquainted with the work of Gordon Allport.[8] He was a practising Christian and churchman, as well as being a prominent psychologist. He differed radically from the Freudians and Jungians in his lack of concern for developmental factors in assessing present problems. He was more concerned with the self-determining capacities in the present as these might influence the future – 'becoming'. In his interest in the present as pointing towards the future, and not simply back at the past, he is quite close to Jung (although Jung also felt the past to be significant); and to Carl Rogers, who believes in the potentiality for change coming from self-determining capacities, encouraged by the right therapeutic environment in the present. Allport also suggests broad categories of personal development, which include the spiritual dimension. There are some similarities here to the more developed model since put forward by Fowler (see V:25).

It is equally valuable to include this extract as a contribution from the Antipodes: its author, Terry Creagh, lectures in pastoral theology in New Zealand.

The Religious Sentiment[9]

Conscious Determinants of Behavior and the Religious Sentiment

Functional Autonomy. Allport was convinced that mature adult motivation has no functional relation to the historical roots of the motive, and functional autonomy in fact permits a relative divorce from the past of the organism. There is no such thing as a fixed personality pattern by reason of early genetic, biological, or developmental factors. As a person matures, he or she makes choices that fit current and future needs and aspirations. 'The history of the individual becomes a matter of relative indifference if he is at present driven by desires and intentions that are independent of what motivated the individual at earlier periods.' Where persons are locked into earlier motivations for action, this is likely to

8. For example, *The Individual and His Religion* (New York, Macmillan, 1950) and *Becoming: Basic Considerations for a Psychology of Personality* (Yale Univ. Press, 1955). Most of the quotations in the extract which follows have been taken from either book, although I have deleted references to save inessential footnotes. The original article is, of course, fully referenced. – Ed.
9. From T. Creagh, 'Gordon W. Allport's Psychology of the Individual: Implications for Pastoral Care' (*The Journal of Pastoral Care*, vol. xxxv, no. 4, December 1981, pp. 250–63).

reflect the 'repetition compulsion' pattern of neurotic behavior. Under normal circumstances Allport viewed adult motives as *supplanting* the motives of infancy, and thus he develops his psychology of the supreme uniqueness of human individuality.

Disposition. Human personality is governed very largely by a distinctive individual disposition to realize possibilities. Allport employed the word 'trait' to describe processes and structures which persons *have in common*. But the term 'disposition' carries more weight in describing what belongs to the *individual* person. The disposition is inborn as the raw material for the development of personality yet is never identical in any two people: to help us understand this Allport speaks of 'the Billian quality of Bill'. It is the Billian quality of Bill, or the Jillian quality of Jill, that he was interested in recognizing and knowing. Though people do have dispositions in common (traits), Allport made more of their distinctive and particular dispositions; a person can be 'known' on account of his or her dispositions (note John 10:3 NEB; 'He calls his own sheep by name'); the dispositions describe a person. Here he underscored the Christian theological position of an individual uniqueness which can never be swallowed up, but only completed, through membership in the People of God. Nevertheless, Allport is not far from the error of individualism and at some distance from the Hebrew contribution to the understanding of the corporate identity of the children of God, or the New Testament concept of organic union within the Body of Christ.

Whereas Freud's 'instincts' insure survival, Allport's 'dispositions' (alternatively, 'capacities') insure growth and orderly structure. Also, the emphasis of Allport is upon conscious, rather than unconscious, determinants of behavior in the reasonably well-adjusted adult – a person who devotes most of his or her energies to the future as an extension of the present, instead of upon events of the past. When counselees do little but look backwards to bemoan the circumstances of their past lives, I sometimes encourage them to look to the future by inquiring after their goals, their expectations in life; where would they like to see themselves tomorrow, next year, in ten years' time? Are goals achievable and in line with inherent capacities? Where might the first steps be taken (i.e. task: here learnings from past trial and error may be employed again)? As the new process of becoming is set in motion I must supportively stand by my counselee, taking very seriously what one person described as 'the lonesomeness of changing things'.

Sentiment. Allport says that 'in the course of development relatively stable units of personality gradually emerge' wherever favorable conditions exist. Where the tendency in a person is directed toward some definable object of value, such as mother or fatherland, this becomes a *sentiment*, a constructive attitude of readiness. The sentiment may be abstract, relating to values or beauty; it may be negative, with an aversion to persons, ideas or objects (thus an atheist may have a negative sentiment relating to all things commonly regarded as religious; in this case the object of the sentiment is a 'disvalue' rather than a value). To summarize, for Allport a sentiment 'represents an organization of feeling and thought directed toward some definable object of value . . . when I use the word sentiment, I might equally well for our purpose speak of *interest, outlook* or *system of beliefs.*'

There is a particular *religious* sentiment which Allport defined in this manner: 'A disposition, built up through experience, to respond in favorable and in certain habitual ways, to conceptual objects and principles that the individual regards as of ultimate importance in his own life, and as having to do with what he regards as permanent or central in the nature of things.' This is very broad and universal: the person who makes material possessions central and ultimate in his life, the Christian might regard as an idolater; but this idolater still has a religious sentiment. Even if immature and selfish, the idolater's religion may be all that sustains him or her.

To use a metaphor of Allport's, subjective religion is a white light in personality which, though luminous and simple, is in reality multi-colored in composition. 'The astonishing thing about the religious sentiment . . . is that although it entails many component attitudes and objects of interest, it represents nonetheless a stable unit of mental life. The component attitudes are variable but all contribute to a single well-patterned system.'

A mature religious sentiment possesses a sustaining, driving power in its own right, certainly not limited to the infantile roots of the outlook. There is nothing in the religious sentiment that is fixed once and for all, but a fluidity of movement and energy which carries forward through the adult years, and is probably especially meaningful in those years. We might profitably compare this with the process of perfection that is unfolding in the life of the mature Christian (intrinsic, or task-oriented). 'New religious sentiments are maturing all the time, producing fresh moral zeal, and engendering consistency upon men's purposes . . . not every "must" of childhood becomes an "ought" of maturity.'

Clearly Allport provides us with a theory that underlines the individual's capacity to live responsibly, not driven by childhood compulsions, but using powers of choice; he or she is a decision maker. His thought over all is nearer to the position of Pelagius than Augustine. The person is capable of exercising rational thought and action, performing wholesome 'works', providing he or she is a reasonably well adjusted, mature being. (Allport gives us a psychology of the 'normal' person rather than of the 'abnormal' maladjusted individual; he starts with health rather than sickness).

Allport does not think of the human being as born totally corrupt, or depraved through heredity and utterly dependent upon grace to pluck him or her from bondage; a child is born with great limitations, but has within the seed of possibilities without limit; given half a chance there is nothing to constrain progress in life. One readily feels a sense of encouragement and hope in this view of our kind. . . .

Personal Development and the 'Stages'
. . . Allport sets forth broad categories of reasonably uninhibited, progressive personal development. Basically, there are two theories of personality – one for early childhood, another for adulthood; he does not make a great deal of the in-between phases. However, his stages of development, such as they are, would indicate: (i) a 'body' stage in infancy; (ii) a 'body-mind' stage in later childhood and adolescence; (iii) a 'soul' stage in adulthood, by which is meant wholeness of being, or 'the fully functioning person' – physically, mentally and spiritually.

As concerns the young child, it is the 'constitutional' factors that stand out, rather than environmental influences. Freud, of course, considers the foundations of character to be laid at around three years, with only some modifications in later years. By contrast, Allport sees the early factors as containing only the *elements* for personal potential and the later blossoming of personality. . . .

According to Allport, from adolescence onwards the developing person is acquiring a hierarchy of interests within the matrix of love and loyalties. A 'transformation' is occurring, though this 'does not eliminate primary egoism altogether – not even in a saint'. The self-love of narcissism surrenders to self-esteem which has altruism as its expression. But in reading Allport we do well to understand that when he speaks of overcoming egoism he does not mean to suggest that we should not love ourselves; nor does Christianity teach that we must be self-depreciating.

What Allport terms the 'proprium' includes all aspects of personality that make for unity – such as bodily sense, self-identity, self-esteem, rational thinking, the function of knowing.

This incorporates identification with abstract entities, such as loyalties and moral and religious values. The mark of maturity in the adult is the range and extent of self-involvement in *abstract* ideals.

Allport is unwilling to define personality too rigidly, or according to a system of easily definable layers, and this is attractive. He does well to give a picture of the unitary nature of the individual, even if he does fail sufficiently to deal with the person as social being. . . .

Consistent with the aforesaid is Allport's contrast of the 'must' of childhood conscience (dread of punishment) with the 'ought' of the adult (sense of obligation rather than compulsion); the adult 'ought', rather than being dependent upon a fear motivation, is stimulated by the assurance of love ('because Christ first loved us . . .'). Guilt, for the adult, comes through a violated value and disgust at falling short of the ideal self-image.

Theologically we find corresponding positions – firstly, the legalistic authoritarian 'commandment' type religion which appeals to fear of consequences; secondly, the ethic of the Beatitudes which imply what people *ought to be*, instead of what they *must do*: an enriched quality of being leads to a finer quality of behavior. Adult religion has at its heart the appeal to Love, to strength and possibility more than to threat and prohibition which are indicative of the immature childish state. Pastors must decide which of these alternatives they will seek to reinforce through their preaching and teaching – do they wish to keep their people childish dependents, or allow them the freedom that goes with 'becoming'?

III:16

The psychological challenge to theology and faith is only one in a series of challenges that have been made since time immemorial. In more recent history those challenges have included the scientific (physical and biological), the historical, the psychological and the sociological. Peter Berger ('A Rumour of Angels', Penguin Books, 1971) explains how sociology has challenged pastoral theology, with its more precise information on what people actually believe and practise in their faith; but he adds that the particular discipline of sociology of knowledge has demonstrated how views of so-called reality actually depend upon the social support they receive – or even, in the case of minority groups which become tightly-knit sects, do not receive, so that such groups tend to close ranks and defend their view of reality against all odds. Such relativization casts the same kind of doubt upon absolutes in truth as Freud's explanations of rationalization do from the psychological angle. At the same time, Berger reminds us that modern thinking is just as relative as any other view of reality, and that religion permits a confrontation with the age in which we live from a perspective that transcends the age, thus putting reality as it is currently perceived into context and in proportion.

A fascinating blend of sociology, anthropology, psychoanalysis and psychiatry is found in the work of the social scientist Ernest Becker. In 'The Birth and Death of Meaning' *he explores what we must know about ourselves if we are to deserve the name* homo sapiens, *presenting a general theory of human nature which is potentially liberating. In the last chapter, 'Religion: the Quest for the Ideal Heroism', he writes:*

Religion – the Quest for the Ideal Heroism [10]

Levels of power and meaning

It seems to me that we have, then, evolutionarily and historically, a common problem for men of good will in all fields to work on: in their own lives if they so choose, and in the social and political sphere. Basically, as Max Scheler understood in the brilliant words we have borrowed as an epigraph to this chapter,[11] it is a problem of the identification of idols. To what powers has a man given himself in order to solve the paradoxes of his life? On what kind of objective structure has he strung out his meanings and fenced off his own free energies? As Scheler points out, each person *has* an idea of the absolutely real, the highest good, the great power; he may not have this idea consciously, in fact he rarely does. The idea grows out of the automatic conditioning of his early learning, he *lives* his version of the real without knowing it, by giving his whole uncritical allegiance to some kind of model of power. So long as he does this he is truly a slave, and Scheler's point is that not only is he unconsciously living a slavish life but he is deluding himself too: he *thinks* he is living on a model of the true absolute, the really real, when actually he is living a second-rate real, a fetish of truth, an idol of power.

10. From E. Becker, *The Birth and Death of Meaning* (Harmondsworth, Penguin Education, 1972), pp. 184–96, copyright © The Free Press, 1962, 1971, reproduced by permission of Penguin Books Ltd.
11. The epigraph includes these words: ' . . . . Even without being quite aware of it, man can fill this sphere of absolute being and of highest good with a *finite* content and good which, in life, he treats 'as if' it were absolute. Money, country, a loved one can be so treated. This is fetishism and idol worship.'

We might say that there were roughly four levels of power and meaning that an individual could 'choose' to live by:

1. The first, most intimate, basic level, is what we could call the Personal one. It is the level of what one is oneself, his 'true' self, his special gift or talent, what he feels himself to be deep down inside, the person he talks to when he is alone, the secret hero of his inner scenario.

2. The second or next highest level we could call the Social. It represents the most immediate extension of one's self to a select few intimate others: one's spouse, his friends, his relatives, perhaps even his pets.

3. The third and next higher level we could call the Secular. It consists of symbols and allegiance at a greater personal distance and often higher in power and compellingness: the corporation, the party, the nation, science, history, humanity.

4. The fourth and highest level of power and meaning we would call the Sacred: it is the invisible and unknown level of power, the insides of nature, the source of creation, God.

These levels, of course, are not discrete for most people: most of us live in several of them, and the importance we assign to each level gives the general orientation and dimensions of our self-world. I said that the individual could 'choose' the levels he would live by and it is obvious why I put the word in quotation marks: usually the person doesn't ask himself this basic question: this is decided for him by the accidents of his birth and training and by the energies of his heredity, his constitution. Taken together they *propel* him into a character structure that operates comfortably on certain levels of power and meaning. The great tragedy of our lives is that the major question of our existence is never put *by* us – it is put by personal and social impulses *for* us. Especially is this true in today's materialist, objectifying, authoritarian society, which couldn't care less about a person answering for himself the main question of his life: 'What is my unique gift, my authentic talent?' As the great Carlyle saw, this is the main problem of a life, the only genuine problem, the one that should bother and preoccupy us all through the early years of our struggle for identity; all through the years when we are tempted to solve the problem of our identity by taking the expedient that our parents, the corporation, the nation offer us; and it is the one that does bother many of us in our middle and later years when we pass everything in review to see if we really

62

had discovered it when we thought we did. Very few of us even find our authentic talent – usually it is found for us, as we stumble into a way of life that society rewards us for. The way things are set up we are rewarded, so to speak, for *not* finding our authentic talent. The result is that most of our life is in large part a rationalization of our failure to find out who we really are, what our basic strength is, what thing it is that we were meant to work upon the world. The question of what one's talent is must always be related to how he works it on the world: 'Into what hero-system do I fit the expression of my talent?' It is worked on some combination of the four levels of power and meaning.

If you stay on the first or Personal level for any length of time you must lead a way of life of an eccentric or a hermit, which few can do; even then it is doubtful whether they can do it without the symbols of allegiance or the solid memories of some of the higher levels laid down in early years. The first level for man is unadulterated narcissism: it is pathological and it invites or is already mental illness.

If you extend your allegiance to the power and meaning of the second level you are still very narrowed down to a limited world: you would remain embedded in the family, live what the psychoanalysts so aptly call 'the incestuous symbiosis' or some kind of *'folie à deux'*. . . .

The process that we call 'secondary socialization' takes people onto level three and if you extend only that far you live as most people do today: you broaden out your identity to the full scope of the social world, make a solution of the problem of your career and your social self-esteem; if you give your allegiance to large, humanistic abstractions like science, the development of history or humanity, you transcend yourself sufficiently to give a rich meaning and support to your life.

Scheler, along with the religious geniuses of mankind, would maintain that to remain on level three without proceeding up to the highest one is to fall short of ultimate reality, to live in a world of idols. They would claim that true heroism for man could only be cosmic, the service of the highest powers, the Creator, the meaning of creation. Thereby you take your authentic talent, what is deep down inside you, your depth and your subjectivity – which is invisible, personal and a mystery to us, and you link it to the highest level – which is also invisible, often personal and a mystery. You take your special secret separateness and you make it ultimately meaningful by linking it to the mysterious service of creation, you draw a full circle on yourself, heal the rupture of your loneliness and isolation. By serving the highest power you serve the best power, not any second-rate one; by linking your destiny to that of creation you give it its proper fulfilment, its proper dignity, its only genuine nobility. . . .

Thus some of mankind's most beautiful and compelling thoughts about the problems of levels of power and meaning. Obviously there is no sure way of knowing these things. As the illustrious William James put it, who himself believed in the desirability of extending one's allegiances up to the highest level: anything less than God is not rational (given the miracle of creation); anything more than the abstraction 'God' (i.e. possession of certain know-ledge about the actual Creator and His plan) is not possible. . . .

But again, if we can't know the real in any objective way, we can at least know what is false to our lives, to the forward-momentum of our conduct. This is a viable, relativist, pragmatic criterion in personal life just as much as it is for the life of a whole society. . . . That is why the first task of psychotherapy is to free the person from other people's opinions. . . . This is why thera-pists often put such a low valuation on the mind, on thought processes: the mind is the social self, the ways we have learned of attuning our self-esteem to the expectations and valuations of others; the mind automatically channels our self-esteem into society's roles. . . . The value of deriving one's power and meaning from the highest level of generality is that it makes this task for the self-esteem easier: one can feel that he has ultimate value deep down inside just by serving in the cosmic hero-system: he has a sense of duty to the very powers of creation and not principally or only to the social world. . . .

Homo heroica
The ideal question for religion grows out of this reality to the human condition, a reality that psychoanalytic science also divulged and shocked our sensibilities with: Roheim said that culture, the marvellous pageantry of the human drama, was the fabrication of a child afraid to be alone in the dark. The ideal question for religion has always been a derivation of this: 'What kind of fabrication would be proper to an adult *who realized that he was afraid*?' In this way religion questions the reality of the heroic task for man, in opposition to the cultural fiction of the heroic. . . .

But we saw too, in chapter 11, that the psychoanalytic view was not complete, that the child reacts not only to the threat of despair but also to the overwhelmingness of the miraculous. Both of these dimensions of experience dwarf him and threaten his power and sanity. And so we can understand why the religious ideal is potentially the most liberating for man: it reflects the twofold reality of his situation, the problem of despair as well as the problem of miracle; and it leaves man open to devise ever-new and creative solutions to that reality. . . .

Yet these evolutionary abstractions can be of little immediate comfort to us, even though they represent ideals that seem grounded in hard empirical fact. If we talk about the highest level of meaning and the ideal of religion and science as one of openness, we get no automatic blessing for belief and no firm pedestal for hope. Our situation remains the same, torn by the same fundamental paradox: *individuality-within-finitude*, self-consciousness and emergence from nature, yet boundness to nature and to death. This is why the religious phrasing of this paradox, the myth of the Garden of Eden which occurred so early to man, still serves us today. Man was once on a par with all the rest of nature, blissfully ignorant of his condition and his fate. But then he 'ate the apple' of self-knowledge: and felt 'shame': that is, he now had self-reflexivity and self-consciousness, he 'stuck out' from all the other animals and could no longer enjoy their serene existence, their ignorance of death and of the burden of the miraculous. . . .

From all this we conclude that the contradictions of man's earthly situation cannot be resolved by easy belief or by reflexively relaying the meaning of it to God. Genuine heroism for man is still the power to support contradictions, no matter how glaring or hopeless they may seem. The ideal critique of a faith must always be whether it embodies within itself the fundamental contradictions of the human paradox and yet is able to support them without fanaticism, sadism and narcissism, but with openness and trust. Religion itself is an ideal of strength and of potential for growth, of what man might become by assuming the burden of his life, as well as by being partly relieved of it.

III:17

If the present enthralment with psychology at times provokes the justifiable complaint that pastoral counselling tends to neglect the pastoral care of society and its structures, it is plain from some of the readings already included that some of the anthropologists and sociologists who have taken psychoanalysis seriously do not neglect more global (or, more accurately, Western) cultural problems. These are equally important areas for pastoral theology, difficult though it may be to make definitive statements about such value-laden issues. Heije Faber, a Dutch pastoral theologian, reminds us that the crisis in modern Western culture is reflected in modern theology itself; a crisis no doubt that has been partly fuelled by the psychological critique, but one to which he suggests psychoanalysis may have two contributions to make:

The Identity Crisis in Theology [12]

In the sphere of theology too all kinds of things are astir and with a view to our discussion we must try to explain the points – often fundamental ones – where there seems to be uncertainty. Our partners in the discussion would otherwise not be in a position to carry on a real discussion with us.

I do not think that I am viewing the present crisis of theology (and the churches) in unduly simple terms when I say that the uncertainty proclaimed itself in the last century with Kierkegaard. In the atmosphere of confidence, general as well as ecclesiastical, which prevailed in those days, he tried by his activity to draw attention to an element of inescapable insecurity. This uncertainty could be generally sensed during the First World War and afterwards. . . . The theologians who raised their voices during the Second World War and afterwards seemed to extend the uncertainty to tradition and the church as well. Bultmann's de-mythologizing and Bonhoeffer's recognition that the people of our time (ourselves included) are no longer responsive to the tiny residue of 'religion' within ourselves, destroy a series of supports for human life which have helped for centuries to overcome the unbelief that dwells in the midst of all belief. In his book *Honest to God* the Anglican Bishop Robinson expresses the feeling that he is bound to testify to a great uncertainty in the inner centres of his faith. With this he seems to accentuate an uncertainty which fills tens of thousands and which in its inarticulate form is apparently experienced as a crushing load. Tillich too has shown that most religious words and images have lost their power and that we have to try to make their content our own in a new way and using new words. The image of God is no exception. We have to learn to find God in the depths in 'the shaking of the foundations', or we shall not find him at all any more. Another American theologian, van Buren, maintains that in the gospel we really only have to do with Christ, the man in our own human history. Many plead for a faith 'in the horizontal', or urge that we should find it in love of our fellow men.

12. From H. Faber, *Psychology of Religion* (London, SCM Press, 1976), pp. 137–42.

A religious crisis such as this cannot be solved by psychological means, but with the help of psychology we can certainly try to make certain aspects of it comprehensible. I myself have no doubt that from the beginning the uncertainty was concentrated on the very centre, on belief itself. Kierkegaard's life was already dominated by the question of what belief really is. His question is: who am I as a believer? Erikson would say that in the present crisis it is a question of the believer's identity. He has taught us that our identity has to do with the society that lends an identity, as well as with an ideology that helps us to arrive at identity. But although society today knows practising Christians, and perhaps also adherents of the churches, it has no pattern, no identity for the believer. We therefore have to achieve our identity by our own methods. But here the church does not supply us with an ideology. It has done this right down through the centuries, through its theology and liturgy; but this ideology – witness Bultmann and Robinson – now has no efficacy; we no longer live from it. And we have no new ideology to give us support and to create a sense of identity. It is true that we are not quite without anything at all. We find support in the vague consciousness that our uncertainty is a good thing because we sense it in others as well, and that this uncertainty can reveal new possibilities of identification. We listen to Bonhoeffer and Robinson, but we also, as it were, listen to what is behind them.

If this is a more or less adequate representation of the situation, it seems to me that there are two important viewpoints with which psycho-analysis, above all, can help us. The first is that uncertainty can only be overcome if it is expressed, and expressed as openly as possible, as it is by Robinson in *Honest to God*. Repressed uncertainty has a destructive effect. We must deduce from the reactions to Robinson's book that in our world a great deal of inner insecurity was repressed by the sense of obligation to conform to the ecclesiastical forms of the day – its forms of liturgy and tradition, the picture people have of faith and the church. The overtone which could be heard in the word faith was evidently '*must*'. Faith and the church are fixed elements in a cultural pattern and this determined the picture which many people have of these two entities. These people certainly know that faith has something to do with a highly personal decision, but the doubt which is essentially bound up with it (and which the New Testament, for example, testifies to) can find no real place in their lives. They do not know how to cope with it, they suppress it, with the result that their faith becomes no true faith at all. For faith has the overtone of 'you *may*' – and here I am convinced

67

that we can learn something very important from psycho-analysis: that the path to true life (and in this case to true faith) can only be found when what is suppressed is made conscious and so enters into relationships with other 'islands of experience'. In this way it can also be expressed and takes on the concrete form essential for conversation and hence for growth and integration, i.e. acceptance and 'use'.

Here we can learn from Luther, from the analysis which Erikson makes of his struggle.[13] According to Erikson (p. 205), Luther first took a step forward when he accepted his doubt, when in a profound sense he dared to be passive, without attempting to hold on to his insecurity with the courage of despair. 'What he had tried so desperately and for so long to counteract and overcome he now accepted as his divine gift – the sense of utter abandonment, *sicut jam damnatus*, as if already in hell.'. . .

I have mentioned the example of Luther deliberately, because I believe that the whole problem of identity, in the significance which Erikson ascribes to it in the context of Luther's struggle, has validity for our own times as well. According to Erikson, Luther did not only find a new identity for himself; he found one for his period as well.

In reality our whole Western world seems to have stuck fast in an identity crisis. Our religious struggle is part of this Western identity crisis. Erikson talks (p. 20) about ideology as the world image which gives a basis for the sense of identity, as the 'unconscious tendency underlying religious and scientific as well as political thought'. For those who have an understanding of these things, the religious crisis reveals a clear relationship to everything that is going on in existentialism as well as in the most widely varying forms of modern life. . . .

In this case the theme of our 'ideology' is not, as it is with Luther, the God-man relationship in the form of justification by faith, not works. And the theme which many of us viewed as the fundamental theme of the twentieth century – the question of the meaning of life – does not seem to me central either. The central theme is rather that we are balanced between liberty and bondage, between authentic existence and inauthentic existence, the experience of being, not as firm ground beneath our feet, but as a dialectical 'letting go' and simultaneous seeking for something to hold on to at the edge of an abyss, where we go on without having any clear direction.

We might now ask: why do we not jump down from our tight-

13. See III:13.

68

rope? It seems to me that the answer must be: because it *has* to be like this, and because we are also balancing between hope and fear, in a mistrustful basic trust that we shall *succeed*, indeed that this balancing act in our relationship to our fellow-men and to God (about whom, however, we can say hardly anything specific) contains within itself unexpected and fearful potentialities.

Psycho-analysis can in my opinion make still one more contribution in this situation. I have already said that psychology cannot solve any religious crisis. That crisis must be solved from the sources over which religion itself disposes: the relationship to God, the thinking through of that relationship, the articulation of doubt, the common search and common prayer, the listening, the being open to the Spirit. But psychology can try to shed light on the situation and make it comprehensible.

We have already said that in the present religious crisis part of our culture's identity crisis is working itself out and that this is comparable with the crisis of Luther's period. This is not chance; there are reasons for it. Can anything be said about these reasons?

Because of my lack of specialist knowledge, I do not feel competent to answer the question, but I would like to point hypothetically to *one* aspect, which I hope might take on a clearer outline through a closer investigation.

What strikes me about the modern theological literature we have mentioned is its rebellion against the aspects of belief and the church which Jaspers so aptly calls the 'shell': the state church with its hierarchy (Kierkegaard), mythology (Bultmann), the fixed premises (Bonhoeffer), the established forms and ideas (Robinson). Bound up with this is the need to accept only what is genuine and what fulfills its function and is not offered as tradition. One needs very little training in psycho-analysis to see that here our relationship to the previous generation is working itself out. But it is not so much healthy resistance towards the 'fathers' that is being expressed; under normal circumstances that leads to a critical appropriation of tradition and thus to a healthy cultural transmission. What we find here is rather an unwillingness, and hence an inability, to identify with the 'fathers'. The 'fathers' give the impression of being shut up in the 'shell'; people do not find in them the living quality of true faith. They do not want the 'shell', but see no chance of identifying themselves with its 'faith'. This leads to the rejection of the shell and, as far as belief is concerned, the need to undertake one's own journeys of discovery in order to find the God in the depths (Tillich), to experiment (like modern art), to be genuine and to accept lack of security as an essential element in the human condition (existentialism). Behind the crisis of these years, therefore, I see the inability of fathers to give their sons the chance for identification. . . . Many people feel that the changes in the theological climate mean a lapse from the path which Karl Barth followed in his theology for so many years. Is this not connected with the fact that his patriarchal type of religion no longer quite fits our gradually changing pattern, in which the 'fatherly' elements have become obscured? In this case the increasing prominence of 'family' aspects (the Lord's Supper, brotherly love, unity) as well as a certain mysticism (the God in the depths, the Oriental renaissance) could perhaps be understood as the chance for receptivity to other elements – *pre-fatherly* elements, as it were, in human development.

We can only say these things very hesitantly. They are highly speculative. But they are in principle capable of verification and can perhaps even, with reservations, make certain developments comprehensible, so helping us to be less strained and more tolerant towards the present and the future.

III:18

To conclude this section, it is appropriate to represent the Jewish contribution to the pastoral care and counselling movement in Britain, and in so doing to highlight the inter-faith nature of pastoral work, where common problems of practice tend to transcend differences of theological belief. Irene Bloomfield, before retirement, worked as a psychotherapist in the National Health Service in London. In the extract that follows I have omitted her case examples and most of her conclusions, which mainly summarize her paper.

Religion and Psychotherapy – Friends or Foes? [14]

In talking about religion and psychotherapy it is important to recognize that there are many schools of thought in both fields. All try to explain the nature of man, and his relationship to the world around him. Whatever I may say, therefore, about either religion or psychotherapy, can be contradicted. All we can do is to look at what appear to be broad areas of agreement, of conflict, and of ways in which each can learn from the other.

It may be that I shall raise more questions that I can answer, but

14. From article with this title: I. Bloomfield (*Contact*, 61, 1978: 4, pp. 3–12).

I hope that these questions will give an opportunity for dialogue. Although I am involved in both, I have no wish to gloss over differences which may exist, but would prefer to look at ways in which conflicts may be reconciled, or acknowledge that there may be some fundamental differences. In talking of religion I am primarily looking at Judaeo-Christian concepts since I have not had enough experience of other faiths.

Joint Concerns
Both religion and psychotherapy are concerned with growth and wholeness, with people's attitudes, feelings and behaviour. Both require self-understanding. Both formulate theories about the general nature of man and the determinants of his behaviour.

Differences
Although there are these joint concerns, there are differences in what we mean by wholeness and growth and the ways in which these may be achieved. Religion does, on the whole, pay far more attention to a specification of norms and standards for behaviour. These are thought to be derived from divine revelation embodied in written and moral law. This means that in the past there has been relatively little ambiguity for the religious person regarding conduct which was considered right or wrong.

Solomon Schimmel in a recent paper on *Judaism and Contemporary Psychology*, states that

> Jewish law spells out in great detail how the individual is expected to behave in almost any situation, whether towards parents, spouse, children, neighbours, strangers, employers or employees. Nothing is left to chance. Guidelines for behaviour are quite definite, and are meant for the lay person as much as for the Rabbi. No individual, therefore, can plead ignorance.

Psychology, on the other hand does not, on the whole, specify how the individual is to behave in any particular situation. Instead, the therapist tends to think in terms of 'realization of potential', 'better adjustment', 'individuation', 'self-actualization' and 'wholeness'. Some therapies include in their aims something about values and meaning, but the nature of these values and meaning may differ from one individual to the next. Other therapies do not take account of any existential dimension and in that differ fundamentally from theological thinking.

Religion tends to start with an image of the ideal to be achieved, of where the individual ought to be or get to. Therapy tends to

71

start with where the individual is at this moment and tries to help him unfold and develop whatever unique qualities he had within.

Wholeness in religion is often equated with holiness, with being 'perfect as the Lord is perfect', with upholding certain values, standards, traditions and religious laws as well as with having a good relationship with God. For the therapist, wholeness means an acknowledgement and acceptance of all aspects of ourselves, including the dark side of our nature, such as anger, bitterness, hurt, envy, jealousy, and hate. The acceptance of this dark side is necessary, not in order to act on these feelings, but because keeping them out of consciousness means that they exercise power over us which is unpredictable and uncontrollable. Many religious people believe that to own their bad feelings would mean that they are not as perfect as they ought to be, and therefore they need to work even harder to push such feelings underground where they become inaccessible. The individual who has to deny so much of himself cannot be a really authentic or whole person, and authenticity is one of the aims of therapy.

Differences in the Concept of Man:

Freedom of Will

According to the Biblical view of man, he is made in the image of God, and therefore has free will to behave in accordance with religious law, and to live the good life, or he can turn away from God and behave sinfully and wickedly. The assumption is that nothing but his weakness or his badness prevent him from becoming whole or holy, and further, that the sinner brings injury upon himself.

It seems to me that such teaching addresses itself almost entirely to the conscious, adult part of the individual which can make such choices – leaving out of account the more primitive, child-self which is an inevitable and important part of all of us throughout our lives.

Most schools of psychotherapy would agree that there comes a point in all our lives where we have to take responsibility for what we are and wish to become. Psychotherapists do not, however, accept the notion that we can simply make decisions about desirable or unacceptable behaviour. They take the view that man's behaviour and attitudes are determined by a combination of hereditary and environmental factors. They believe that patterns of response are laid down early on in life as a result of childhood experience, and frequently continue relatively unchanged into adult situations, where they are no longer appropriate. But

72

because the origins of such patterns go back such a long way, to the time before we could apply our logical minds, they are very deeply ingrained, often hard to understand, and very difficult to change. . . .

So much of our behaviour, our attitudes and our perceptions of the world are determined by childhood experiences. Our first relationships largely determine how we experience relationships with subsequent people and with God.

Injunctions

One of the injunctions that comes to mind is the one about honouring your father and mother. There are people whose experience of parental cruelty, neglect and rejection makes it impossible for them to honour or respect their parents, but for the religious person the failure to do so is just one more piece of evidence that he is now well launched on the way to perdition.

As a therapist I have seen a number of people who were able to forgive their parents' cruelty and neglect when they could understand them better and recognize that the parents too had suffered from their respective backgrounds, and perhaps this understanding and forgiveness is the first step towards 'honouring' parents, but I do not think that people can just make a positive decision to do so until they feel understood, accepted and 'honoured' themselves.

You may say that this happens through confession or spiritual guidance, but frequently that is not how the penitent perceives what happens in the confessional. Acceptance has to be based on real, genuine understanding. It has to be more than outer form. I am not in a position to speak from my own experience, but I am speaking about the way in which many of my patients or counsellees experience confession and spiritual guidance.

As I said earlier, theologians generally act on the presumption that man has the freedom to be good if only he tries hard enough. They do not, therefore, take into consideration the unconscious mechanisms which often give rise to incomprehensible behaviour and irrational emotions – the areas with which the psychotherapist is primarily concerned. . . .

Much religious teaching is concerned with the way people *ought* to feel, like loving your neighbour as yourself, but how can you make yourself love either yourself or your neighbour when you have never experienced love? I gather there are the few who are able to feel loved by God, even though they have not experienced the love of man in the shape of parents or parent substitutes, but I must confess that such people have not come my way, even

73

among clergy and religious. The religious person may say that the individual's self-hatred can be transformed through the love of God, but in my experience he cannot feel the love of God if he has not felt the love of man. Perhaps the gospel writers recognized this when they said in 1 John 4:21, 'Anyone who says "I love God" and hates his brother is a liar, since a man who does not love the brother that he can see cannot love God whom he has never seen.'

This is a truth the therapist comes up against constantly. The child who has never experienced parental love, affection and acceptance cannot feel loving towards other people, or towards God. It is very difficult to enable such a child to receive love from anyone because either he does not trust it or he simply cannot feel it. The prognosis is more hopeful where there has been someone at some point in the child's life who gave him love. This does not have to be a parent. It may be a granny, a foster parent, an older sibling or a nanny. So long as he has experienced love from someone, it is possible to help him find it again in later life, whether in a marriage partner, a friend, a priest, or a therapist. I have to say here, of course, that the therapist may get a somewhat distorted view of mankind because on the whole he sees only those people whose development has been arrested or blocked, thus preventing growth – the clergyman's experience of people may be different. . . .

Authenticity
Much religious teaching and perhaps especially Christianity, does not encourage honesty with ourselves. The recognition that we are not able to meet the most important requirement, that of loving, may be a devastating one.

The question arises: can religion or psychotherapy do anything about this impasse? As I said earlier, one important difference between the two approaches is that religion emphasises what we *ought* to be, think, feel, and do. Psychotherapy stresses the importance of recognizing what we *are*, think and feel at this moment in time. Once we have identified and acknowledged the dark side of our nature, that is, the unacceptable emotions and impulses, they can be modified or transformed; but all the time that they have to be pushed underground because it is too painful and frightening to face them, they remain as a permanent cancer within.

The religious person may deny that much religious teaching encourages us to be dishonest with ourselves and point to confession as an attempt at honestly facing undesirable aspects of ourselves, but the penitent can only face what he knows about. He has no way of getting in touch with those powerful forces within which he has gone to great lengths to push underground and deny to himself. Religious teaching has, in the past, fostered repression of all those apparently unacceptable feelings, like anger, envy, hatred, bitterness, violence, and jealousy, as well as sexuality, because they have not fitted in with the image of the good person, the good Christian, or the good Jew.

This is not to say that psychotherapy encourages people to act on these emotions or impulses. Rather the reverse. Through acknowledging their existence we gain greater control over them. We know what we are fighting. When, on the other hand, impulses are forced underground they are experienced like an underground battalion of assassins who threaten our carefully built citadel or conscience. Much misunderstood psychology has given rise to ideas of permissiveness, laxity of morals and encouragement of violence or sexual acting out. This is far from the truth. It is not the aim of therapy to allow people to act on their impulses. There is instead encouragement to take responsibility for bad feelings as well as good ones, and to substitute inner discipline for external threats. The childhood system of reward and punishment may then give way to internal authority.

Most of the people who come to a psychiatric department have not strayed very obviously from the straight and narrow. They are more likely to turn aggression against themselves rather than against others and to accuse themselves of acts of omission or commission. They are not, on the whole, the people who have committed unlawful acts, but are more likely to be casualities of their own harsh judgement on themselves. A severely depressed person so often is the person who cannot allow himself to express the rage they feel about some hurt which they experienced in the past. The hurt may be one done to them by another person or it may be experienced as having been done by the Almighty, but since they cannot let themselves feel angry with parents or God, they believe that they must themselves be bad and worthless. . . .

[*The author concludes*:]

There is little to differentiate the enlightened practitioner in both fields and indeed there is more common ground between the open-minded therapist and cleric than between the progressives and the more rigid fundamentalists in each discipline. I have tried to identify differences and similarities in our respective approaches and may have exaggerated some of the differences or not properly

75

understood some of the religious approach, but we can only have reconciliation if we have conflict first.

I would like to end with a quotation from Lucien Bouet:

> Anxiety finds its sustenance in the painful events of the past, its occasion in some physical weakness in the present, and its specificity in fears of the unknown. It is the job of the psychological technique to explore the past, that of the physical technique to rectify the present, and that of faith to illuminate the future.

Our task as representatives of Religion or Psychotherapy is to know which to use when.

Part IV

The Nature of Pastoral Ministry

It is clear from the preceding sections that the disciplines of psychology, anthropology and sociology do not uniformly reduce religion and faith to their own terms. Given the possibility that religion and faith are not mere neuroticism nor examples of mainly harmless social deviance – and that they may actually enhance the life of the individual, the good of the community and the vitality of a culture – how does the person who is involved in pastoral care and counselling differ from her or his secular counterparts? Is there more to their care and counselling than simply being paid by the Church, or working in a church setting? This section of readings seeks to inform some of these questions.

IV:19

Guntrip addresses the question of role in the next extract. He was a minister of the then Congregational Church, who became a very distinguished psychotherapist and writer. Presumably he includes himself as one of those who for whom the exception can be made, not to have to stay in the ministry. He certainly made a very important contribution to British psychoanalytic developments, and brought the thinking of the Scottish analyst W. R. D. Fairbairn to a wide audience.[1] (Fairbairn read classics and theology before medicine and training as an analyst.) Nevertheless, for all his eminence, it is easier for those who are working, as it were, at headquarters (in universities and seminaries; or with a small and select group of clients – and here the editor must include himself) to reflect upon the philosophy, strategy and tactics of pastoral ministry. It is another matter to be engaging these issues on the front line. Only the reader so engaged will truly be in a position to judge whether the following pastoral theologians or psychotherap-

1. See H. Guntrip, *Personality Structure and Human Interaction* (London, Hogarth Press, 1961); *Schizoid Phenomena, Object Relations and the Self* (London, Hogarth Press, 1968); or more simple as an introduction to Guntrip's work, *Healing the Sick Mind* (London, Unwin Books, 1964).

ists have anything of real value to say about the distinctive nature of their own pastoral ministry.

Ministers or Therapists – the Pastor's Role [2]

Whereas psychotherapy is the specific treatment of neurosis and must remain related in the closest way to medicine, pastoral and social psychology is the application of the best modern psychological knowledge to the normal work of the ministry or of social service, to increase the efficiency of the handling of human problems, and deepen insight into, and understanding of, human nature. These two spheres of interest cannot be absolutely separated in theory, nor even altogether in practice, but a fairly clear distinction can and must be made between them for practical purposes.

Naturally, a minister who is a born psychotherapist is in a unique position to discover his inborn powers. Churches will need to recognize such men, and help them to get proper training. But we do not want to turn every minister or social worker into a psychotherapist, even if all were suitable, for who would then do their own proper work? It may not be out of place to consider the fact that some over-discouraged ministers, feeling that the Church as at present constituted is failing to meet the needs of men and women in this restless age of transition, might be tempted to turn to psychotherapy as a way out of the sinking ship. After all, ministers are human, and are liable to feel, in their own particular setting, the pressure of security-motives and prestige-motives that operate in people elsewhere. Ministers not infrequently suffer from the feeling that their profession is accorded scant respect in the world generally, and seek to sustain their sense of their own value and obtain recognition from others by branching out into some not directly ministerial activity. Needless to say, this is not a sound motive for taking up psychology. In fact, of course, a minister is accepted everywhere at his real value as a man, and if he is worth his place in the ministry he will be respected and his help sought by all kinds of people who might never think of going to a church service. There is no position that has greater strategic value or offers more infinitely varied opportunities of practical service to men than that of the Christian minister. It is urgently necessary, not only for the Church but for

2. From H. Guntrip, *Psychology for Ministers and Social Workers* (London, George Allen and Unwin, 3rd edn, 1971), pp. 40–3.

the community, that there should be ministers as fully equipped as possible, not only spiritually but scientifically, to do their work.

A minister's job, then, is primarily to be a minister, to minister to the emotionally, intellectually, and spiritually storm-tossed men and women and young people of this confusing period of history. All around are folk whose minds are being eaten into by scepticisms, cynicisms, doubts and fears, whose faith in human nature, in themselves, in God, is being undermined by a sense of helplessness and hopelessness, who are hungry for convictions, yet in danger of drifting into the feeling that life has little or no meaning. *Here is the minister's field, not in working with those who have broken down with neurosis, but with those who are carrying on bravely, if often very anxiously, in the midst of the pressures and puzzles of a disturbing and confusing social, cultural, political and international scene. . . .*

A psychotherapist's business is primarily to restore a nervously ill person to working capacity and to adjust him to his fellow men. That latter part of the task is, of course, a profoundly religious aim. . . . Adjustment to the finite and the infinite, to man and God, are interrelated and inseparable, but that does not warrant us in merely identifying the two. The work of the minister goes beyond that of the psychotherapist into the region of the ultimate issues and meanings of human existence. That is the real reason why we do not want simply to turn every minister into a psychotherapist.

There is also a practical reason, namely, that it is impossible to run a highly organized and busy church that caters for the needs of children, young people, adults, and old folk in a many-sided life, and at the same time carry on a full practice in psychotherapy. Sooner or later one or the other must suffer, and a man has to choose. By far the great majority of ministers ought to choose first and foremost to be ministers; only here and there will a man be pushed inexorably along the path of psychotherapy in a specialist way. After all, the ministry is itself as much a speciality as psychotherapy. . . .

What use, then, can a minister make of psychology in the course of the normal work of pastoral visitation, receiving people who come to seek help and advice, and preaching? . . . the chief directions . . . may be summarized as: (1) understanding character; (2) religious problems; (3) preventive work; (4) relieving simple anxiety states.

Most of the pastoral theology which relates to pastoral counselling comes from the United States – although continental work in this area exists, but remains largely untranslated; for example, Joachim Scharfenberg, a German Professor of Practical Theology and a trained analyst. I have included here two important exceptions to the American dominance of the market – a comment upon the Lutheran pastoral theologian Eduard Thurneysen, and an extract from the British pastoral theologian Alistair Campbell. Pastoral theology in Britain has not by and large fully turned its attention to counselling, except as a phenomenon of which there is a certain amount of suspicion (Part Six). Pastoral care, of course, consists of much more than counselling, and the wider issues in pastoral care are those which theologians tend to address.

Edward Thornton, a major American figure, provides here an example of theology of the pastoral ministry, with particular reference to the pastoral conversation:

The Purpose of Pastoral Ministry [3]

We now shift our focus from the clinical situations from which theological conversations emerge to the theological statements with which clinical work is both informed and reformed. I begin with a definition of the purpose of pastoral care and counseling and move to a statement of faith. *Pastoral care and counseling are forms of religious ministry which integrate the findings of behavioral science and theology in the effort to prepare the way for divine–human encounter in the midst of human crises.*

Any statement about the purpose of pastoral counseling presupposes a statement of faith. This is true because the purpose of a pastoral function cannot be defined theologically apart from the purpose of the church and of ministry in all its forms. The purpose of the church and of ministry presupposes a theological understanding of the purpose of God in the world. And a statement about the purpose of God in the world is an affirmation of faith. In order to offer a theological viewpoint concerning the purpose of pastoral care and counseling, I must begin with a statement of faith and work back to the proposition stated above.

What is God's intention toward us? *God intends to meet us*

3. From E. E. Thornton, *Theology and Pastoral Counseling* (Philadelphia, Fortress Press, Prentice-Hall, 1964), pp. 27–37.

with salvation in every experience of life! . . . The possibility of
divine–human encounter is particularly real in the crisis experiences of life.

Every human experience is potentially revelatory. The ground
of meeting between God and men is not fenced by ecclesiastical
or dogmatic barriers; it is not prescribed by sex, race, class or
nation; the prerequisite for divine–human encounter is neither a
particular psychological disposition nor a state of emotional and
physical health. Consciousness and rationality are not the sole
grounds for this decisive encounter. . . .

But is it not contradictory for us to say that the ground of
meeting between God and man is not fenced and then to say that
God meets us in Jesus Christ – in the continuing incarnation of
Christ in the church? A contradiction exists if we think of the
church exclusively in terms of formal, religious affiliation and if
we think of the church only as it is gathered for worship and
instruction. If we think also of the church dispersed in the world,
serving the world in the name of Jesus Christ, we may perceive
Christ in the most unlikely places – meaning the most irreligious
communities and the most ordinary experiences. The parable of
the sheep and goats (Matthew 25:31–46) teaches us that some
men will discover that unbeknown to themselves they have been
on God's side all along. . . .

God's intention is to meet us not only in emotional health but
also in mental illness. For thousands of years mental illness was
understood to be a form of demon possession. Then in 1920 a
minister named Anton Boisen suffered a mental illness. Four
years later, Boisen became a full time Protestant chaplain in a
mental hospital. He, more than any other person, has awakened
us to God's intention to meet men in mental illness as well as in
mental health. Boisen understands his own illness as a religious
experience. At stake were issues of spiritual life and death. While
still a patient, he saw that the functional psychoses of many patients around him were manifestations of religious as well as of
medical problems. Mental illness is one's response to the disorganization of one's inner world. A death, an acute disappointment
or a pervasive sense of failure may trigger the disorganization.
The illness becomes a way both of denying or concealing one's
feelings and of confessing them and crying for understanding and
help. One may withdraw, drift or fight in response to the disorganization of one's inner world. But God's intention is to meet,
sustain and deliver the sufferer from his isolation and disinte-
gration. If demons are involved in mental illness, we ought not

81

to speak of demon possession but of demons *being engaged by God* in the life of an individual. . . .

God's intention is to meet us not only in consciousness but also in our unconscious mental processes. Specifically, God meets us in our dreams. Jacob fled from his enraged brother, Esau, and in sleep 'he dreamed . . . and Jacob awoke from his sleep, and said, Surely the Lord is in this place; and I did not know it' (Genesis 28:12, 16). Had Jacob understood God's intention in a way characteristic of many modern believers – including most ministers – he would have rubbed his head and muttered about the wild dreams which disturbed his sleep. Then he would have pulled himself together to face the rigours of the day ahead without giving his dream life serious thought. . . .

God's intention is to meet man not in isolation but in the context of a community of faith. . . . The uniqueness of the Hebrew-Christian understanding of God inheres in the particularity and concreteness of the community in which God discloses himself. . . . *The theme of divine–human encounter is to be understood throughout this discussion as a reference to encounter within community not in isolation from one's community of faith.* . . .

We may return now to the proposition set forth in the opening paragraph of this chapter. The purpose of pastoral care and counseling is to *prepare the way for divine–human encounter* in the midst of human crises. What is the content of divine–human encounter? Toward what does this language point? The content of divine–human encounter is the forgiveness of sins, the experience of grace. It is salvation and sanctification conceived of as inseparable aspects of a continuing experience. It is man's discovery that he exists before God and that God, who once was feared, may now be freely trusted and loved. The apostle Paul speaks of being 'justified by faith' (Romans 5:1) and of being 'reconciled' to God; he defines Christian ministry as the ministry 'of reconciliation' (2 Corinthians 5:19–20). Paul Tillich speaks of the courage to accept acceptance. Eduard Thurneysen says, '*the* question with which pastoral care is concerned is this: "Do you know that all your sins are forgiven you in Jesus Christ?" '[4]. . . .

To define the content of divine–human encounter as the communication of grace or the forgiveness of sin is one thing. To prepare the way for such an encounter is quite another matter. To know the ultimate word in theological terms does not equip one to communicate it effectively in existential relationships. The

4. See IV:21.

purpose of pastoral care and counseling is only superficially defined if we ignore the clinical realities toward which the theological statement points. The preparation of the way for the communication of divine grace is an extremely complex task deserving the utmost in professional competence and religious commitment.

The complexity of the task inheres in the nature of man – in what may be described theologically as man's struggle against grace. In general hospital ministry I am impressed by the tenacious way many patients hold that the meaning of their illness is a punishment for sins. . . .

How does one communicate the Word of grace to a person who clings to the feeling that his illness is a punishment for sins? Reading the Scriptures, reasoning about one's theology and even prayer fail to modify the attitudes of most patients. The pastor's dilemma is that his words are not effective in communicating the divine Word. Even reciting the Scriptures fails to effectively communicate the Word of forgiveness and reconciliation. . . . How does a minister effectively communicate to his parishioner the feeling 'God loves me – I am loved!'

This is our dilemma. We have not defined the purpose of pastoral care and counseling until we have defined both the content of divine–human encounter and the process by which a pastor prepares the way for this decisive encounter. Perhaps, then, deeds will communicate where words fail. . . .

We act as if grace were not enough in the religious life, as if gratitude were a weaker motive for ministry than competition. Character guidance and religious education display a similar distrust of the effectiveness of grace. Here the appeal to duty, to the keeping of the law, is often employed more vigorously than the communication of acceptance. Forgiveness presupposes judgement. Law must be known and respected – and violation confessed – before grace can be received. But if grace is not experienced, the religious life crushes us instead of setting us free.

How, then, shall we understand the purpose of pastoral ministry? If it is to be understood as a preparation of the way for divine–human encounter in which grace is communicated and reconciliation experienced, in what sense does the pastor prepare the way? Are his techniques of listening and acceptance more effective than his reading of Scriptures and offering of prayer? Perhaps his task is to speak about the ultimate Word with little regard to the quality of interpersonal relationship between himself and his parishioner. May we place an absolute value upon either alternative or a combination of both? Should the pastor make his message explicit or rely on its being implicit in the pastor–parishioner relationship? Is any method or combination of methods ultimately effective in preparing the way for divine–human encounter? These questions call for a comparison of the methods of pastoral care and counseling with other methods of ministry within the church and with the methods of the helping professions outside the church.

IV:21

The reader may have noticed (and may or may not have welcomed) the shift in emphasis in the extract from Thornton, which makes it totally different from nearly all that has been used in the book to this point. Here God actually gets a mention! The stress is on what can be discovered about God, and not simply about persons. There is a meeting with the divine, which is more than the meeting between two persons which counselling may be thought to be. The divine–human encounter takes place within the community of faith – no isolation here from the rest of the Church. This major change (scarcely surprising, since after all theology is Thornton's principal concern) is equally evident in Thurneysen, an obviously Lutheran theologian, who shifts the emphasis of the pastoral conversation even further, so that the pastor listens not only to the life situation presented to her or him; but also listens for the Word of God that must be addressed to that situation. I now summarize some of Thurneysen's argument.

Listening to the Word of God [5]

On one level, Thurneysen sees pastoral conversation as about a human situation, but pastoral conversation also means a type of acceptance that both comes from and leads to the Word of God. So although this means full engagement with the actual situation which is presented to the pastor, it also means that he or she has to remain true to the significance of God's place in all aspects of human life. Conversation, in other words, must point towards God as the main source of help, and it may then 'bear fruit'.

Thurneysen provides two examples: one might be a dinner conversation in which it is necessary to speak from a Christian

5. Eduard Thurneysen's view of the pastoral conversation can be found on pp. 124–9 of his *A Theology of Pastoral Care* (Richmond VA, John Knox Press, 1962).

84

position, *although not through preaching; preaching may be as much a betrayal of the Word as silence. But bearing witness is important. His other example is more in the counselling vein, where a couple sent by a psychiatrist to the pastor want help which is more than a mere extension of psychological knowledge. If they come to a pastor they expect insights based upon and communicated by the Word of God. It is important to recognize that nowhere does Thurneysen deny the value of psychological understanding, but rather he points to the danger of stopping at such a worldly aspect and losing sight of the true task. 'The Word wants to become flesh, or rather the incarnate Word wants to speak here and now to men who, in the entanglement of their lives, no longer expect to hear additional psychological advice and human counsel, worthwhile as they may be; they long to receive light and truth from the word of God in such a way that they understand it, that their sins are disclosed to them and their forgiveness made known.'*

Thurneysen certainly puts his finger on a dilemma which many psychologically-trained pastors face; which is how to remain true both to their psychological understanding, and to their religious position, but without imposing their views upon the other person, since this is the antithesis of good counselling. Thurneysen makes his position clearer when he emphasizes the need to hear *or* listen, *which again includes careful attention to the human situation, as well as listening to the voice of God's Word for that situation. 'Such listening to man and attention to the Word of God is the true characteristic of the hearing which is at the heart of pastoral conversation.' That he disowns preaching is made clear by his suggestion that such listening may go on throughout the whole session, without the pastor making more than clarifying remarks.*

What is frustrating is that Thurneysen gives us no clear help in how to achieve this balance between the listening with which counsellors are familiar, and the listening to the Word of God, which he confidently states will contain, if we can perceive it, the 'answer to our neighbour's problem'. He does suggest studying the writings of true pastoral counsellors; and also advises listening in the pastoral conversation as we do nowhere else. This is a listening which, in his words, is 'controlled, obedient hearing . . . that comes very close to prayer' *(his emphasis).*

One reason for his inability to give detailed advice is that this ability to hear cannot be gained through training, but has to be given to us, springing from the love of Christ. He suggests that the way to attain it is to be more diligent in 'association with the Word of God' *(his emphasis). Understanding people means studying scripture, which contains the key to the innermost secrets of mankind. While the pastoral counsellor cannot ever know enough of the field of human psychology, unless it is under the guidance of scripture any other education is of no help to the pastoral counsellor.*

IV:22

Thurneysen's position is too much for Thornton (see also IV: 20)! Thurneysen goes too far – although it is interesting to note that Thornton's editor, in the foreword to 'Theology and Pastoral Counseling' *thinks that Thornton is too hard on Thurneysen!*

Who Has the Last Word? [6]

Is it possible that Thurneysen is the victim of a split between his theology and his practice of pastoral care? I think he is. . . .

Thurneysen begins as the defender of the sovereignty and freedom of God. He contradicts himself by limiting the work of the Holy Spirit to the realm of a pastor's proclamation of the Word of God. This appears in several themes.

The contradiction appears first in defining pastoral care and all other pastoral functions as variant forms of proclamation. Thurneysen warns against the reification of the Holy Spirit in the hierarchical system of Roman Catholicism. He is inattentive, however, to the danger of the reification of the Holy Spirit in the traditional words of Protestantism. . . .

The contradiction is implicit, also, in Thurneysen's insistence upon pastoral authoritarianism. He assumes as much authority for the spiritual welfare of his parishioners as a medical doctor assumes for his patients. The pastor must both diagnose and prescribe. Analogy between medicine and pastoral care is not valid at this point. In the spiritual life the pastor participates as fully as the parishioner in the ambiguities of life. The pastor is not above sin. He is more like than unlike his troubled counselees. The authoritarianism of Thurneysen assumes that the pastor has a perspective on the life of his parishioner that is almost identical with God's perspective. Nowhere does Thurneysen make room for the pastor to acknowledge to his parishioner his own bondage

6. From E. E. Thornton, *Theology and Pastoral Counseling* (Philadelphia, Fortress Press, Prentice-Hall, 1964), pp. 52–3.

to hostile and erotic feelings, to mixed motivations, to insecurity and anxiety.

Thurneysen describes pastoral care as pastoral conversation. He allows no real conversation to occur. In true conversation, a pastor risks real engagement. He risks real change in himself as a result of the conversation. He is emotionally prepared to be met by God in his conversation partner. Thurneysen speaks of this risk, but he does not, in fact, take it. He warns pastors about the danger of pastoral arrogance. But, unfortunately, he encourages arrogance by handing over too much authority to the pastor.

IV:23

There is a clear contrast in style between that of the extracts above (IV:20–22) and that of Alistair Campbell. He certainly knows American pastoral theology and therapy first-hand, and is one of the few British pastoral theologians who is well known to American pastoral theologians.[7] The Thornton/Thurneysen arguments concentrate upon explicit theology, fitting the practice of pastoral counselling or pastoral conversation into that framework. Campbell starts rather with images, and explores those images through literature, sacred and secular, and through psychological insights. The theology therefore comes through to the reader in the form of metaphor and parallel, through poetry and evocative use of Word and word. In this extract the image is the journey, but other important images for Campbell are the shepherd (pace Siltner and others), the wounded healer (pace H. Nouwen, 'The Wounded Healer', New York, Doubleday, 1979) and the fool.

The Journey [8]

We come finally to the problem of faith. The mystery of our lives is not as easily solved as we might think in those heady moments when the joy of liberating grace fills our hearts. Certainly grace opens a new vision, gives fresh courage. Yet the problem of faith remains. Our lives continue through many difficulties and uncertainties, and the struggle to make sense of it all goes on:

7. See also A. V. Campbell, *Moderated Love: A Theology of Professional Care* (London, SPCK, 1984); *Paid to Care* (London, SPCK, 1985); *The Gospel of Anger* (London, SPCK, 1986).
8. From A. V. Campbell, *Rediscovering Pastoral Care* (London, Darton Longman and Todd, rev. edn 1986), pp. 82–3, 90–7, used by permission of the publishers.

'We wait for God to make us his sons and set our whole being free' (Rom. 8:23 TEV). So faith often falters and the bright hope coming from our moments of release from sin's cavern can seem like an empty dream. For this reason, traditional pastoral care has always stressed the need to nourish and strengthen faith throughout a person's life. Each of us has a pilgrimage to make on a road which is strangely familiar, though we know we have never trodden it before. We find ourselves on a journey, beginning at birth, ending at death, whose destination we only dimly understand. We know we are searching for something, yet the nature of the thing we seek constantly eludes us. On this strange journey, in this tantalizing search, we often feel lonely and bemused, in need of guidance, encouragement, companionship. Not always knowing what we are asking, we reach out for the help of others to lead us back to faith.

JOURNEYING AND SEARCHING

As we begin to think more carefully about this problem we shall realize that metaphors like 'searching' or 'journeying' are somewhat inadequate for describing the quest for faith. There are senses in which faith can never be found by a search, however persistent, nor reached by a journey, however long. As we shall see later in this chapter, our strivings and wanderings are often the biggest impediments to faith. Faith comes when we cease our restless quest for it. Faith is the beginning, as well as the end, of the journey. Yet, paradoxically, the journey and the search are also part of the experience. Only in movement do we experience the repose of faith, just as it is only against the dark that we can perceive light. . . .

[*Campbell illustrates the image of the journey from Hesse and Bunyan; and the image of the search from the writing of Maslow and Erikson (see III:14 and III:13 respectively). He then moves on to*:]

FAITH AND COMPANIONSHIP

Nothing could be more arrogant than to suggest that we ourselves have finally 'arrived' on this journey of faith – unless it is to set ourselves up as the expert route-finders for others! Of course we can often see when we (and others) have gone wrong, have wandered off the way that leads to our true peace. But to *find* the way again (not in outward conformity, but in inner truth), that is infinitely harder. I have already suggested that the idea of companionship may be the best means of describing that subtle relationship of caring which opens the way back to faith. I shall now suggest three modes of such companionship: sharing bread on the road to faith; sharing repose in the midst of the journey; sharing danger at journey's end.

Sharing Bread

The root meaning of 'companion' is 'he who shares bread'. This has significance at several levels. At the simplest level it means that we are one with others in our fellow humanity. Like them, we must eat to live and, even in the most sophisticated of us, the fight for survival is only a little below the surface. It is out of this knowledge of fear and fragility that we support others in word and action when faith seems far away. If we manage to speak to their fear it is because we know it ourselves and make ourselves no better than they in pointing it out. If we manage to comfort their sense of loss, it is only because the loss strikes to our heart, and starts tears in our eyes. Thus companionship is a way of understanding why people get caught up with 'proximate' goals, with the temporary security of popularity, fame, success. But the good companion also knows, from personal experience, that 'man does not live by bread alone' (Deut. 8:3; Mat. 4:4). He or she has found in life the living bread (John 6:51), the bread from a loving Father freely given if only we ask for it (Mat. 7:9), the bread broken in love for us (Mat. 26:26). So the good companion 'shares bread' in the sense of helping people to transcend the anxiety about material things, which can ultimately give them no peace. The essential *equality* of companionship must remain however. As soon as a needy person senses a vantage point of spiritual superiority, the smugness of a faith without doubt, he or she will feel once more alone in their search. . . .

At a second level, the 'sharer of bread' enters the other's life for a while. . . . Yet the true companion is also someone who avoids making oneself indispensable to the other or becoming parasitic on the other. This again must be true in words and in actions. We can only share in someone else's life search if we are prepared to expose ourselves a little, speaking about things which matter deeply to us as well as the other and risking ourselves in service of the other. But our companionship fails if our words dominate *the other's* search or if our actions remove *the other's* need to journey on.

At a third level 'sharing bread' denotes a communion which sustains and transcends the companionship. All discipleship of

Jesus is companionship in this sense. As Jesus shared bread with his disciples, so he told them to remember him with the same common sharing (1 Cor. 11:24f). He told his disciples that only two or three needed to be present in his name for him to be present also (Mat. 18:20). . . . Such companionship is not to be confused with an anxious seeking out of the company of the like-minded in order to protect ourselves from too challenging a confrontation in life. The true companion often begins as a stranger. In giving a welcome to such strangers we may entertain angels unawares (Heb. 13:2), for, in the words of St Patrick, we shall often find Christ 'in the mouth of friend *and* stranger.'

Sharing Repose
Companionship is also the sharing of repose. People who seek companionship on faith's journey are often unaware that their greatest need is for a friend who will refuse to take their anxious striving too seriously. The companion, who is also a good friend, is capable of mediating that atmosphere of faith so well described in a sermon of Paul Tillich's:

> It is as though a voice were saying: 'You are accepted, *you are accepted*, accepted by that which is greater than you, and the name of which you do not know. Do not ask for the name now. Perhaps you will find it later. Do not try to do anything now. Perhaps later you will do much. Do not seek for anything, do not perform anything. Do not intend anything. Simply accept the fact that you are accepted.'

. . . . The companionship which is also friendship knows the virtue of doing nothing and so freely offers a fellowship of inactivity, an encouragement to repose. The experience of worship (where this has not been corrupted by our anxious activism) provides the pattern for such openings for faith. Worship is sharing time with a friend. The Sabbath which is truly made for man gives us release from the need to work. The day of the Lord's resurrection puts a time of hope and joy at the beginning of every week. The rhythm of the Christian festivals offers release from the treadmill of a life measured by productivity. Praying together, singing together, being silent together, listening together: these components of worship are the sounds and silences of a warm friendship, where 'hearts are open . . . no secrets are hid', where time can be spent with a God who henceforth calls us not servants but friends (John 15:15). Such friendship is often hard to find in long-established churches, in which worship has become an *activity*, sustained out of a sense of obligation to a God who demands regularity. In such places the dusty and disorientated traveller feels ill at ease, an outsider disturbing the stately routine of God's more diligent worshippers. So the friendship of God and the friendship of humanity must intertwine, and for all of us the repose of true worship comes only when we are able to relax in the company of those who, for a little while at least, have come close to us, shared our journey, sought with us somewhere to rest.

Comradeship of Journey's End

Finally, companionship on the strange journey of faith must at times become *comradeship*. The comrade is needed when mortal danger looms. He or she stands by my side, facing a darkness which may engulf us both. In the image of the comrade we recall the courage of the shepherd who enters the dark valley, the bleeding of the healer who knows mortality, the crazy loyalty of the Fool which makes him enter the night's dark storm. Comradeship is needed when the reality of death is too much for us to bear. Even the most courageous, the most trusting and the most faithful of us can find it hard to gaze calmly into the face of death. For death brings such catastrophic losses. It threatens all that is familiar to us: places where we feel at home, the often unnoticed habitation of our own body, the touch and sound of those we love. Death presents faith with its greatest challenge, because it suggests that there is nothing to hope for, nothing to gain in journeying on, when in the end there is only loss, blankness, extinction:

> This is a special way of being afraid
> No trick dispels . . .
> . . . this is what we fear – no sight, no sound,
> No touch or taste or smell, nothing to think with,
> Nothing to love or link with,
> The anaesthetic from which none come round.

The companion who sees no such threat in death will be useless as a comrade at journey's end. Faith is not strengthened by the denial of death's enmity. (Philip Larkin, in the poem quoted above, believed that religion, 'that vast, moth-eaten, musical brocade', was merely a pretence that we never die.) But by a mere denial of death faith is insidiously weakened, since such denial prepares us poorly for the anger, fear and grief which bereavement and our own mortality bring. We can call death 'kind and gentle' like St Francis, but only because 'Christ the way hath trod', a comrade going ahead into the cold unknown to lead us home. The enmity of death lies in its finality. Whatever lies beyond it, whether it be darkness or light, it means the ending of life as we have always known it. . . .

The comrade, then, is a fellow-soldier who helps us fight a common enemy. She or he does this by taking our anger and our fear with the utmost seriousness, not by making us feel ashamed of such emotions or by offering a 'religious' consolation which denies the affront of death. But the comrade *is* a fighter, who strengthens our determination that death shall not have the final victory. Such determination is needed not only when death is imminent (for, after all, many of us will die suddenly, with no prior warning); rather, it is a confrontation with powers of darkness which is needed throughout our earthly days. When we shrink from such a direct gaze into the face of death, we live half-lives, trivializing human relationships, inhibited from a full expression of our powers by our terror of the unknown. The good comrade on life's journey will not allow us to diminish ourselves with such evasions and useful defences. . . .

The need of the helper and the helped are one: in life, in death in the midst of life, we can give and receive care only by discovering those things which alone enable us to stand firm against every threat to faith. The courage which is demanded of us is not the fearlessness of those who trust in their own physical, mental or emotional strength. The courage to fight the dark powers comes from the integrity of the person who trusts in truth and peace, who reaches out for salvation and faith, whose only weapon against despair is the inspiration of God's spirit. Thus the end of the journey of faith is not, as we often suppose, a stepping out of the world into a disembodied, deathless life. On the contrary, the vanquishing of the powers of darkness, reveals the strangest of all mysteries. The end of our journey has been with us from its very beginning: in our life, in our bodies struggling to find peace in their world, in all our wanderings, searchings, journeyings, we have never been separated from the totality of love, which is God (Rom. 8:37–39).

IV:24

The particular discipline which the pastor brings to care and coun-
selling is the theological: for some theology will be in the more
formal style expressed in the examples from Thornton and Thurney-
sen above; others will prefer the style that is seen in the extract from
Campbell. Whatever its expression the theology of the pastoral
conversation also has to be translated into the actual practice of

pastoral care and counselling, from the over-arching or under-pinning theological dimensions to the human situations and the personal dilemmas which particular persons bring to the pastor for her or his advice or help.

In addition, there is a further distinctive role which the pastor, ordained and lay, has in care and counselling, because he or she is one who is expected to speak the language of spiritual growth. Some who are attracted to the fresh, and culturally more acceptable, language of the psychologist and counsellor are not sure how to integrate the language of spirituality, fearing (with some justification) that people will not understand, or may even be put off by the more traditional language of the spiritual director.

Yet the pursuit of spiritual growth need not be foreign to the pastoral counsellor, as Howard Clinebell demonstrates in 'Basic Types of Pastoral Care and Counseling', probably the most influential of the American books in this field currently available in Britain. Written originally in 1966, and passing through several editions, Clinebell has revised and updated his text, including for the first time recognition of the growth of lay caring groups, environmental concerns, liberation theology and feminism. These subjects merit more attention than this reader can give; instead I remain with this reader's central theme, with passages from the chapter 'Facilitating Spiritual Wholeness: the Heart of Pastoral Care and Counseling'.

Facilitating Spiritual Wholeness [9]

The Spiritual Dimension in All Human Problems
In certain types of problems the religious-existential aspects are obvious and pressing. According to Erik Erikson[10] youth in later adolescence are highly exposed to problems of their basic identity and, therefore, to existential anxiety. It is no accident that schizophrenia frequently begins at this time. Spiritual issues are prominent in the crisis of the middle years, when one's youthful illusions of physical immortality crumble before the realities of aging. Psychologist Herman Feifel has discovered that 'a primary subconscious concern of the person over fifty, as revealed through projective testing, is preoccupation with his own death'. Existential-

9. From H. Clinebell, *Basic Types of Pastoral Care and Counseling* (London, SCM Press, 1984), pp. 106–20. See also R. T. Barnhouse, 'Spiritual Direction and Psychotherapy' (*The Journal of Pastoral Care*, vol. xxxiii, no. 3, September 1979, pp. 149–63.
10. See III:13.

religious factors are often near the surface in crises counseling, particularly in counseling with the sick, the dying, and the bereaved. Their crisis experiences crack the defensive shell of pseudo-omnipotence that most of us wear, confronting us with the brevity and vulnerability of our lives, and forcing us to be aware of the clock that relentlessly ticks away, bringing us closer to the grave moment by moment.

Though often not so obvious and in some cases completely hidden, there is an existential-spiritual dimension in *every problem* with which pastor and parishioner struggle in counseling. This is true because awareness of our mortality is inherent in every human experience, most often on a subconscious level. . . .

Paul Tillich points out that the threat of nonbeing producing existential anxiety has three forms – the threat of fate and death, emptiness and loss of meaning, guilt and condemnation. This anxiety permeates our whole being. It is a part of our 'heritage of finitude', the dark shadow touching all other anxieties and giving them their power. . . .

There are no psychological or psychotherapeutic answers to existential anxiety. It is existential in that it is inherent in our very existence as self-aware creatures. But *its impact on the individual can be either creative or destructive*, depending on how it is handled. Whatever one uses to cope with existential anxiety is, psychologically speaking, one's religion. This may be one of the many forms of idolatry – the deification of possessions, health, success, alcohol, the state, an institution such as a church, one's family, making these matters of 'ultimate concern' (Tillich). Neurotic problems can also be understood as defenses against nonbeing, attempts to avoid existential anxiety. Ironically, the use of these defenses inevitably produces precisely what is feared – nonbeing. That is, the neurosis lessens a person's aliveness. Tillich views neurotic anxiety as a way of avoiding the threat of nonbeing by avoiding being (defending oneself against the fear of death by feeling half-dead). . . .

The only constructive means of handling existential anxiety is an authentic religious life, enabling the actualization of the image of God within the person. . . . Life-enhancing religion enables persons to confront rather than evade their existential anxiety. As Tillich made clear, only as this normal anxiety is confronted and taken into one's self-identity can it enhance instead of cripple life. . . .

The Goal of Counseling on Religious Problems
The goal of the religious dimension of pastoral care and coun-

seling is to help people grow in the depth and vitality of their spiritual life so that it will empower all aspects of their lives. This growth occurs as they learn to relate to God, people (God's children), nature (God's world) and their own inner being in ways that satisfy nine basic spiritual needs – the need for: (1) developing a viable philosophy of life; a belief system and living symbols that give meaning to their lives; (2) developing creative images and values to guide their life-styles constructively; (3) having a growing relationship with and commitment to a loving God that integrates and energizes their lives; (4) developing their higher self (Assagioli) or soul as the center of their whole being; (5) renewing regularly their basic trust (Erikson[11]) to maintain hope in the midst of the losses and tragedies of their lives; (6) discovering ways to move from the alienation of guilt to the reconciliation of forgiveness; (7) developing ways to undergird self-esteem and reduce alienating narcissism (pride) with an awareness of being deeply valued by God; (8) having regular moments of transcendence, mystical 'peak experiences' (Maslow[12]) when they experience the eternal in the midst of time; and (9) belonging to a caring community (e.g., a church) that nurtures and sustains them on their spiritual journey. . . .

It is crucial to be aware of the spiritual crisis on our planet. This is the context of the spiritual longings, confusion, and emptiness that people bring to the counseling pastor. It is a difficult time to satisfy our deep spiritual hungers constructively. The unprecedented speed of social change has produced a massive collapse of traditional systems of religious beliefs, symbols, meanings, and values for millions on planet earth. Traditional authority-centered ways of handling existential anxiety and satisfying spiritual needs are no longer acceptable or meaningful to them. But they have not yet developed new, more creative ways. This time of radical spiritual transition is saturated with existential anxiety for many people. Some flee from the freedom (and the necessity) to develop more creative spirituality by turning to simplistic, authoritarian religious 'solutions' espoused by pseudo-messiahs. In Erich Fromm's[13] term, they 'escape from freedom' to reduce the anxiety aroused by our planet's spiritual crisis. A subconscious awareness of this crisis is one factor that brings people to counseling pastors.

When viewed through the glasses of growth, this spiritual crisis confronts humankind with an unprecedented opportunity (and

11. See III:13.
12. See III:14.
13. See III:12.

95

need) for spiritual transformation. When we let go of comfortable answers that no longer satisfy, we are confronted by the necessity to 'work out [our] own salvation with fear and trembling' (Phil. 2:12). Those who question authority-validated beliefs and values are confronted by the need to discover beliefs and values that make sense *to them*. The process of putting away childish but comfortable beliefs (see 1 Cor. 13:11) is painful, but it is an essential part of the process of growing up spiritually. Spiritually-oriented pastoral counseling can provide valuable help to people in their search for spiritual wholeness in our contemporary spiritual crisis.

Pastoral counseling on spiritual issues aims at helping people learn to live in harmony with the basic principles of the psychological-spiritual world, as these are understood in the Judeo-Christian tradition. To align one's life-style with this fundamental spiritual reality is what is meant in religious language by 'doing the will of God'. Pastoral counseling seeks to help people enjoy an open, growing relationship with God, enabling them to live growthfully amidst the losses, conflicts, and tragedies of life in the world. It seeks to help them become aware of the exciting fact that they are made to be active partners – co-creators with the Spirit of the universe in transforming the world. Pastoral counseling seeks to help persons renew their sense of basic trust by being in touch with the Spirit of love present in this moment, to find healing of those aspects of their brokenness that can only be healed in relationship to this reality. Pastoral counseling aims at helping persons find their vocation – their calling, their cause – into which they can pour their lives with purpose, commitment, and joy. . . .

As persons discover and develop those spiritual capacities that are their transpersonal essence – the higher Self within them – their existential anxiety is gradually transformed into a constructive force in their lives. Persons who treat themselves like machines, who feel they have never lived, whose inner creativity and aliveness are trammeled by neurotic conflicts tend to be most terrified by death. Conversely, persons who have learned to stay open to the loving Spirit of life and thereby come alive within themselves, find that awareness of their finitude is transformed into a stimulus for living more fully and purposefully. The more the image of God is developed within them, the more they can participate in the 'celebration of being' (Bugental). Our most basic alienation as human beings is from the transcendent within us. To discover and develop this image of God is the key task of spiritual growth work.

Persons in the mid-years who suddenly realize, 'My life is more than half-gone!' experience a wave of existential anxiety. (I remember the first time I was hit by this awareness!) If their lives have a spiritual vacuum, they may feel overwhelmed. If, on the other hand, their sense of meaning is undergirded by a viable faith and a robust spiritual life, they can transcend the shackles of finitude. The process of aging is transformed. Rather than live dying, they will die living! Obviously there are important implications in this for counseling with those in their mid-years and beyond.

Diagnosing and Treating Spiritual Problems
Facilitating spiritual wholeness in pastoral counseling involves recognizing and understanding the particular spiritual problems of the person, then using appropriate methods to bring healing to that brokenness. When persons talk in counseling about aging and death, the meaning or meaninglessness of their lives, their responses to sickness and crises, their when-the-chips-are-down beliefs, their guilt feelings – usually they are asking for help with spiritual issues. Often the cry for such help is less obvious. It is disguised as dull purposelessness, empty longing, chronic boredom, or simply lack of zest and inner joy in living. The pastor's goal is to lead such persons toward an awareness of the underlying spiritual and value roots of their dilemmas in living. There are two levels in the process of much counseling – helping persons deal with their immediate problems or crises, and then encouraging them to examine the underlying value-spiritual issues of which their current problems are painful symptoms. If ministers help persons handle their immediate problems, they have done only half of their job, though an important half. The other crucial task is to help persons face the deeper problems of inadequate meanings, distorted or destructive values and life-styles that are the hidden sources of many of their problems in living. The spiritual growth opportunities potentially present in the problems that bring persons for counseling are often missed because people are not encouraged to explore the spiritual roots of their crises.

A pastor should not be timid about raising diagnostic questions regarding spiritual issues and the need for spiritual growth. Here are some examples of 'opening questions' a counselor can use to invite people to explore spiritual issues:

'How do you understand this decision in light of what's most important in your life?'
'How does this problem with which you're struggling relate to your personal faith, to your relationship with God?'

'What have you learned from the miserable crisis? Has it changed your faith?'

Questions of this type should be asked only after a trustful relationship is established and the pressure of coping with the acute phase of a crisis is reduced. So timed, they may open doors for constructive dialogue about underlying spiritual issues such as unresolved guilt feelings and magical beliefs that persons need to replace with a more reality-respecting faith. Such dialogue can help people find meaningful answers to the big questions – 'What does my life mean?' 'What is the quality of my relationship with God?' 'Is my life-style (and the values it reflects) destroying what's precious to me, including my health?' A man who had suffered a severe health crisis declared, after such a discussion of value and life-style issues, 'As long as nobody asks the big questions, you can ignore them and let them be. But once they're asked, you can't put them down until you have an answer.' People are more likely to find meaningful answers and to grow spiritually if they have the help of a spiritual guide as they wrestle with such difficult faith issues.

The diagnosis of spiritual pathology and the identification of areas where spiritual growth work is needed can be facilitated by using criteria such as these:

DO THE RELIGIOUS BELIEFS, ATTITUDES, AND PRACTICES OF PERSONS

– give them a meaningful philosophy of life that provides trust and hope in facing the inevitable tragedies of life?

– provide creative values and ethical sensitivities that serve as inner guidelines for behavior that is both personally and socially responsible?

– provide an integrating, energizing, growing relationship with that loving Spirit that religions call God?

– nurture the transcendent dimensions of persons' lives, their higher Self?

– inspire an ecological love of nature and a reverence for all life?

– provide for a regular renewal of basic trust by affirming a deep sense of belonging in the universe?

– bring the inner enrichment and growth that comes from 'peak experience'?

– offer the person a growth-enabling community of caring and meaning (e.g. their church)?

– build bridges rather than barriers between them and persons with differing values and faith systems?

– enhance love and self-acceptance (rather than fear and guilt) in their inner life?

– foster self-esteem and the 'owning' and using of their strengths in constructive living?

– stimulate the growth of their inner freedom and autonomy?

– help them develop depth relationships committed to mutual growth?

– encourage the vital energies of sex and assertiveness to be used in affirmative, responsible ways rather than in repressive or people-damaging ways?

– foster realistic hope by encouraging the acceptance rather than the denial of reality?

– provide them with effective means of moving from the alienation of appropriate guilt to healing reconciliation with themselves, other persons, and God?

– encourage creative development in their beliefs and values through the life cycle to keep these congruent with their intellectual growth?

– provide effective means of keeping in touch with the creative resources of the unconscious through living symbols, meaningful rituals, and vital myths?

– encourage them to keep in touch with both the soft, vulnerable, nurturing, receptive, feelingful side *and* the assertive, rational, intentional, ethically demanding side of their personalities and their religion?

– make them aware of person-hurting institutional practices and motivate them to work to change these forces that oppress potentializing on a massive scale?

– give them the trust, hope, and meaning to face their awareness of death and the inevitable losses of life and to allow their awareness to make living more precious?

– keep them aware of the basic wonder and mystery of all life and growth?

– encourage heightened aliveness, joy, celebration of the *good gift of life* and an increasing commitment to living creatively – as an instrument of wholeness in response to this gift?

These criteria have evolved over the years from my observations of the ways personal religion can enhance or diminish human wholeness in all dimensions of people's life. As a working hypothesis, I hold that to the extent that one's religious life meets criteria such as these, it will enhance wholeness-centred-in-Spirit. To the extent that it does not meet such criteria, one's religious life will diminish wholeness. These criteria can be used in self-diagnosis by persons in counseling or in growth groups to help them identify areas where they need to focus their spiritual growth work. The criteria can be presented with the suggestion that they be used to evaluate one's own spiritual health. The criteria all refer to different facets of one reality – the vitality and wholeness of one's spiritual life. They are stated broadly so that they can be applied to the spiritual dimension of any individual's life, whatever her or his religious orientation or traditions.

Part V

Faith and Personality

Whether we lean towards the strict Freudian criticism of religion, or the more positive views on the significance of religion that have questioned Freud's negativity, faith and religion clearly express in some form the ultimate concerns of persons generally, and specifically of those who offer a ministry of pastoral care and counselling. Religion and psychology address similar issues, with psychology to date perhaps assisting in the task of distinguishing authentic and inauthentic religion rather more obviously than religion has yet helped distinguish authentic and inauthentic psychology. From all this it follows that faith development and personal growth go hand-in-hand, like Campbell's companions on a journey (see IV:23).

V:25

As it is, faith development has so far been poorly addressed in British care and counselling literature. Frank Lake is the sole representative in the selections that appear in this part. In fact American pastoral counsellors have been almost as pre-occupied with the practical issues of training, supervision and accreditation, and have only fairly recently turned their attention to faith development, as the dates of the following extracts show. Notwithstanding William James's analysis of religious personality types, or the work of Gordon Allport (see III:15), it is James Fowler who has placed this subject more firmly on the map of research, even if his work still has to be accommodated to pastoral practice. Fowler's 'Stages of Faith', presents a model of faith development which draws together theories put forward by Erikson (See III:13), Kohlberg and Piaget – all referred to in the extract that follows. Fowler has followed up this presentation of his research with a chapter in 'Clinical Handbook of Pastoral Counseling', which one reviewer feels is a more relevant presentation of faith development for clinicians.[1]

The Dynamics of Faith[2]

Wherever I lecture or speak about faith development research I meet people who suggest that I should choose some other term to describe the focus of this work. I find the variety of substitutes they suggest interesting; I find their protests against using the word *faith* instructive. Several groups of critics have a deep suspicion that the concept of faith is really inseparable from religion and belief. . . . They reject the claim that faith is a generic feature of the human struggle to find and maintain meaning and that it may or may not find religious expression. Their proposed substitutions for faith go in two directions. Those who are favorable to religion and who would like to see this kind of work be fully identified with the scientific study of religion feel that I would be more honest if I simply described it as research on religious development. On the other hand, persons who fear that the linkage of faith and religion taints or limits the usefulness of an otherwise promising body of theory urge that I take the opposite direction. They suggest the use of some more strictly secular term for our focal concern. They have proposed 'world view development', 'belief system formation', or, on occasion, the 'development of consciousness' as categories that would help us avoid confusion.

Two other quite different groups oppose our use of faith for understandable reasons. One of these groups are the Christian critics, particularly those who are heirs of Protestant neo-orthodoxy's stringent commitment to the Reformation's stress on faith as solely the gift of God's grace, given uniquely in Jesus Christ. They protest that we are misusing the term. They claim that faith is an indigenously Christian category and that it owes its proper understanding to Luther and Calvin's reinterpretation of St Paul's theology. Psychological critics, on the other hand, argue that what

1. Fowler and Osmer, 'Childhood and Adolescents – a Faith Development Perspective', in R. J. Wicks, R. D. Parsons and D. Capps, *Clinical Handbook of Pastoral Counseling* (USA, Paulist Press, 1985). See also Fowler's *Becoming Adult, Becoming Christian: Adult Development and Christian Faith* (San Francisco, Harper and Row, 1984).
2. From J. W. Fowler, *Stages of Faith – The Psychology of Human Development and the Quest for Meaning* (Copyright © 1981 by J. Fowler. Used with permission from Harper and Row Publishers, Inc., San Francisco), pp. 91–3, 98, 106–10, 310–12.

we call faith and the stages we present here might with less confusion be designated as *ego* and as stages of *ego development*. . . . They tend to believe, as do the Christian critics, though for contrasting reasons, that our concept of faith is too broad and inclusive.

Our use of the term *faith* does make many people uncomfortable. As Harvey Cox once said to me, 'There is something to offend everyone in this way of talking about faith!' Yet I think we cannot afford to give up faith as our focal concept despite its complexity, its likelihood of being misunderstood, and the difficulty of pinning it down precisely. There simply is no other concept that holds together those various interrelated dimensions of human knowing, valuing, committing and acting that must be considered together if we want to understand the making and maintaining of human meaning. . . .

In the most formal and comprehensive terms I can state it, *faith* is:

People's evolved and evolving ways
of experiencing self, others and world
(as they construct them)

as related to and affected by the
ultimate conditions of existence
(as they construct them)

and of shaping their lives' purposes and meanings,
trusts and loyalties, in the light of the
character of being, value and power
determining the ultimate conditions
of existence (as grasped in their
operative images – conscious and
unconscious – of them).

This characterization of faith is, I will grant, formidable in its formalism. Immediately I must ask you to recall all that we said earlier about faith as social and relational. You must give flesh to those definitional bones by calling to mind the variety of communities with and in which persons go about composing (or recomposing) self, others and world in light of their relatedness to shared images of an ultimate environment. Let your remembering include communities as disparate as the devotees of Krishna consciousness, the Jonestown cult in Guyana and the committed adherents of an Enlightenment rationalism all convened in a recent university symposium. Let the flesh you bring to this formal characterization of faith include the 'civil religion' of a veteran's organization, the revolutionary fervor of a black liberation movement in southern Africa and the quiet serenity of a Zen Buddhist monk who has attained *satori*.

But consider the virtues of our formal characterization. It does, I believe, capture the essential triadic dynamics of faith. Wherever we properly speak of faith it involves people's shaping or testing their lives' defining directions and relationships with others in accordance with coordinates of value and power recognized as ultimate. . . .

Among the most important contributions of the Piaget-Kohlberg school to our project is its broadly *epistemological focus*. Epistemology has to do with the study of *how* we know. A strong theme in the theological writings on faith of H. Richard Niebuhr and Paul Tillich has to do with faith as a way of *seeing* the world. Faith for them *is* a kind of knowing, a constructing of the world in light of certain disclosures of the character of reality as a whole that are taken as decisive. Different faiths are alternate modes of being in the world that arise out of contrasting ways of composing the ultimate conditions of existence. Ways of *being* and ways of *seeing* are reciprocal. As Niebuhr puts it in *The Responsible Self*, we shape our actions and responses in life in accordance with our interpretations of the larger patterns of actions that impinge upon us. Communities of faith are communities of shared interpretations. The previous section's discussion of the triadic dynamics of faith should have made clear how crucial a part knowing, as the construction of self, others, world and ultimate environment, plays in faith as we study it. The broad epistemological emphasis in the structural-developmental theories serves us well as a model for understanding faith as a way of knowing and interpreting. To make it serve adequately, however, we have to widen the scope of knowing involved and account for the interrelatedness of several different modes of knowing in faith. . . .

From the beginning Erikson's account of stages or eras and the emergent crises which typify them has served as an important framework for our studies. Initially I was inclined to hypothesize stages of faith that largely paralleled Erikson's eras. After encountering the structural-developmental theories, however, and after coming to terms with their more rigorous understanding of structural stages, I began to change the focus of my effort to find stages of faith. I and my associates began to rely on Erikson's theory more as a background against which to hear and analyze the life stories that persons shared with us. We began to realize that a time of movement from one of Erikson's eras to another frequently correlated with or helped to precipitate a change in the structural operations of faith. *But not always.* More recently we have come to see that a person's structural stage of faith (correlated with other structural aspects) has important implications for the way the person will construct the experience of crisis that inaugurates a new Eriksonian developmental era. . . .

Almost as fundamental for our work as Erikson's theory of the developmental eras and their virtues has been his own understanding of and attention to faith. His account of the crisis of the first stage, basic trust vs. mistrust, avowedly deals with the foundations of faith in human life. Erikson carefully avoids any heavy-handed determinism of the sort that would suggest that everything decisive for faith occurs in the first twelve or the first sixty months of life. But he does make plain how powerful a factor the quality of the child's first mutuality with the conditions of his or her existence and with those who mediate the ultimate environment is for all that comes thereafter in identity and faith. In a remarkably suggestive subtheme of his book *Young Man Luther*, Erikson, carefully avoiding the reductionism that marks the work of Freud and many Freudians on these matters, suggests some of the universal features of religious images of God that have their infantile origins in the child's experiences with his or her parents.[3] His attention to *fidelity* as the virtue emerging in adolescence and the accompanying attention to ideology as the young person's necessary concern for finding a comprehensive 'world image' provide access to other central aspects of faith. The study of identity crisis and resolution, through the reshaping of images of faith by young Luther, opens ways to understanding the interplay of faith and culture as well as many other rich issues. Erikson's representation of ethical development in terms of widened care and more inclusive identity contributes an important set of criteria for growth in faith as well as in moral action. Avoiding the trap of identifying faith with religion or belief, Erikson suggests something of his overall orientation toward faith with this statement.

Each society and each age must find the institutionalized form of reverence which derives vitality from its world image. . . . The clinician can only observe that many are proud to be without religion whose children cannot afford their being

3. See III:13.

without it. On the other hand, there are many who seem to derive a vital faith from social action or scientific pursuit. And again, there are many who profess faith, yet in practice breathe mistrust both of life and man.

[Fowler goes on in the major part of his book to describe the different stages of faith, illustrating each with examples from his 359 research interviews. Any summary of the stages is bound to be inadequate, and the interested reader really needs to refer to the original text for a description of the keynotes of each stage, which are:

Stage 0: trust, hope and mutuality;
Stage 1: intuition and projection;
Stage 2: literalism;
Stage 3: conventional faith moving to personal view;
Stage 4: tension between individual and group, self and others;
Stage 5: bringing together opposites and ironies;
Stage 6: experience of life as in tune with the transcendent.

It is perhaps valuable to include the interview guide used in the research (Appendix A in 'Stages of Faith'), which can usefully be compared with Clinebell's questions on religious faith and attitudes (see IV:24); and which might even be used as background questions to have in mind in the practice of pastoral care and counselling:]

FAITH DEVELOPMENT INTERVIEW GUIDE

Part I: Life review
1. Factual data: Date and place of birth? Number and ages of siblings? Occupation of providing parent or parents? Ethnic, racial and religious identifications? Characterization of social class – family of origin and now?
2. Divide life into chapters: (major) segments created by changes or experiences – 'turning points' or general circumstances.
3. In order for me to understand the flow or movement of your life and your way of feeling and thinking about it, what other persons and experiences would be important for me to know about?
4. Thinking about yourself at present: What gives your life meaning? What makes life worth living for you?

Part II: Life-shaping Experiences and Relationships
1. At present, what relationships seem most important for your life? (e.g. intimate, familial or work relationships).

2. You did/did not mention your father in your mentioning of significant relationships.

   When you think of your father as he was during the time you were a child, what stands out? What was his work? What were his special interests? Was he a religious person? Explain.

   When you think of your mother . . . [same questions as previous]?

   Have your perceptions of your parents changed since you were a child? How?

3. Are there other persons who at earlier times or in the present have been significant in the shaping of your outlook on life?
4. Have you experienced losses, crises or suffering that have changed or 'colored' your life in special ways?
5. Have you had moments of joy, ecstasy, peak experience or breakthough that have shaped or changed your life (e.g. in nature, in sexual experience or in the presence of inspiring beauty or communication)?
6. What were the taboos in your early life? How have you lived with or out of those taboos? Can you indicate how the taboos in your life have changed? What are the taboos now?
7. What experiences have affirmed your sense of meaning in life? What experiences have shaken or disturbed your sense of meaning?

Part III: Present Values and Commitments
1. Can you describe the beliefs and values or attitudes that are most important in guiding your own life?
2. What is the purpose of human life?
3. Do you feel that some approaches to life are more 'true' or right than others? Are there some beliefs or values that all or most people *ought* to hold and act on?
4. Are there symbols or images or rituals that are important to you?
5. What relationships or groups are most important as support for your values and beliefs?
6. You have described some beliefs and values that have become important to you. How important are they? In what ways do these beliefs and values find expression in your life? Can you give some specific examples of how and when they have had effect (e.g. times of crisis, decisions, groups affiliated with, causes invested in, risks and costs of commitment)?

7. When you have an important decision or choice to make regarding your life, how do you go about deciding? Example?
8. Is there a 'plan' for human lives? Are we – individually or as a species – determined or affected in our lives by power beyond human control?
9. When life seems most discouraging and hopeless, what holds you up or renews your hope? Example?
10. When you think about the future, what makes you feel most anxious or uneasy (for yourself and those you love; for society or institutions; for the world)?
11. What does death mean to you? What becomes of us when we die?
12. Why do some persons and groups suffer more than others?
13. Some people believe that we will always have poor people among us, and that in general life rewards people according to their efforts. What are your feelings about this?
14. Do you feel that human life on this planet will go on indefinitely; or do you think it is about to end?

Part IV: Religion
1. Do you have or have you had important religious experiences?
2. What feelings do you have when you think about God?
3. Do you consider yourself a religious person?
4. If you pray, what do you feel is going on when you pray?
5. Do you feel that your religious outlook is 'true'? In what sense? Are religious traditions other than your own 'true'?
6. What is sin (or sins)? How have your feelings about this changed? How did you feel or think about sin as a child, an adolescent, and so on?
7. Some people believe that without religion morality breaks down. What do you feel about this?
8. Where do you feel that you are changing, growing, struggling or wrestling with doubt in your life at the present time? Where is your growing edge?
9. What is your image (or idea) of mature faith?

V:26

Since Fowler's model is a developmental one, it is difficult to avoid the implication that a person who has reached Stage 5, for example, is more mature than a person who is still in Stage 4. Admittedly he recognizes that few people move into Stage 5 before mid-life, and that very few people indeed ever achieve Stage 6. Contrast this

developmental model with Joan Hemenway's statement in the article
that follows, where she makes it clear that she does not put forward
her scheme with the assumption that one of the four faith frame-
works is any better than another. She also adds a dimension to her
analysis which is less obvious in Fowler, that of the theological
premises which support a faith framework.

Four Faith Frameworks [4]

I have presented these frameworks to several groups of basic and
advanced CPE [5] students as well as to field education students.
Each time participants have found the scheme helpful because it
is both simple and easy to remember. Their first and primary use
of it has been in examining their own theological orientations and
assumptions in order to discover areas of enjoyment, growth,
inconsistency, blockage and discomfort. Secondly, as with the
original workshop group, presentation of the material has stimulated participants to deal with their differing theological orientations. In the CPE context it has often served to de-personalize
or de-fuse potentially volatile relationships and thus begin more
creative, dispassionate dialogue with one another. Third, it has
helped students sort out some of their own theological history and
baggage, thereby making possible some decisions about what to
keep, what to discard, what is too heavy, what is too light, what
is missing, etc. Fourth, it has given participants an organized way
to think about their own pastoral work with patients and families
and members of congregations, particularly in terms of the theological orientation and consequent pastoral needs of others.

In sharing these frameworks I usually draw four columns on
the blackboard with a heading for each, and then as the material
is presented I urge participants to fill in themes as they recognize
their own theological, ethical or pastoral approaches. In this way
I get to know the participants better, learn how they are reacting
to the material, and benefit from the richness of their thinking
and experience.

The attitude with which I came to this material is essentially an
imaginative, playful one. Since a good deal of stereotyping, brief
characterization and oversimplification about major theological
themes is necessary in order to form each framework, it is
important that the task be approached with an open, creative,

4. From J. E. Hemenway, 'Four Faith Frameworks' (*The Journal of Pastoral Care*,
vol. xxxviii, no. 4, December 1984, pp. 317–23).
5. i.e. Clinical Pastoral Education.

non-defensive mindset. This is an exercise in curiosity, necessitating a good dose of non-literal thinking. As such, consideration of the frameworks is more an act of faith than a presentation of fact.

Framework No. 1: After the Fall

The basic focus for this first framework is the belief that we all live after the fall in the midst of tragedy, sin and evil. Through an unforeseen act of deception, humankind has left the garden of paradise forever behind and is forced to wander and labor in a difficult and godforsaken world. In this framework God is viewed primarily as a Judge who punishes, as a Power not very amenable to the hopes and needs of humanity. Creation is not good; sin is abundant. Jesus, as part of the human situation, is 'a man of sorrows and acquainted with grief'. Death is viewed as inevitable and negative, synonymous with darkness and evil. In this framework there is a great need for rules because human freedom has proven to be disastrous. Theologically it is a view reminiscent of the dark mood of the middle ages when rigid ecclesiastical structures held human evil at bay. It also echoes the fire and brimstone of the New England Puritans, as well as the dire predictions of the apocalyptic literature.

Our main religious experience in this model is one of alienation and separation from God, and inadequacy before God. We feel guilty for what we have done to ourselves and helpless to do anything substantial about it. We wait for better days to come, perhaps only after death, though we are not sure even about this. Ontologically we live in a state of non-being. Psychologically we are bound by our own repressions and suppressions brought about by trying to protect ourselves from the destructive forces within and without (à la Freud). In our worst moments we tend to feel sorry for ourselves as victims of a power beyond our own reckoning. *The Book of Job* and the stoicism of the preacher in *Ecclesiastes* catch the mood of scepticism and hopelessness, and the underlying anger. Pastoral care in this model consists primarily of efforts to offer comfort (*albeit* cold comfort) as we huddle together in the inevitable isolation which is our lot.

Framework No. 2: Jesus Saves

This second framework is based on the central belief that Jesus has saved the world. It is clearly a response and rebuttal to Framework No. 1. By entering into our sinful situation Jesus Christ has redeemed it and us. Therefore, our task in life is to proclaim the Good News that humanity is saved. Through our proclamation of this Word, Jesus' saving work continues alive and operative. God is not so much Judge as He is a Father who sent his only Son, a Redeemer who has given us the Messiah. Death has been overcome, for the promise of eternal life has been received. Though life on earth lived in finite time is not totally good or easy, it is at least fundamentally improved. The cosmic power of evil has been banished and, as a result, our alienation from God has been overcome.

If there was a great need for rules in the first model, in this one there is a great need for faith. This viewpoint sets the scientific (secular, humanistic) world clearly over-and-against the religious (faithful) world. If the doctrine of the fall predominated in Number 1, the importance of Christology (and especially the doctrine of the atonement) predominates here. Pastoral care is seen primarily as evangelism, spreading the Good News which heals the breach between God and humanity. The prophecies of second Isaiah are important as well as the Gospel story and the Pauline letters with their emphasis on what Jesus Christ did, or won, for us. Many would say this is the heart, the truth, the crux of the Christian faith. The charismatic movement and television evangelists give new impetus and fervor to this view among many believers today.

Framework No. 3: God in History
The major emphasis in the third framework is the idea that God has intervened in history, making a special covenant with Israel (and later with the church) to which He remains faithful no matter what. Thus, God continues to intervene in our lives and hearts and history now. As faithful people we live somewhere between the 'already' and the 'not yet' of salvation history. As there was a great need for rules in the first model and a great need for faith in the second, in this framework the central need is for relationship. In fact, pastoral care is defined primarily as reaching out to friends and strangers in ways which make God's presence known and lively. This is how we are to 'keep the promise' of God's love active in the world. Life is a dynamic process within which God is pre-eminently Sustainer. There is a strong doctrine of the Holy Spirit in this model where even 'a still small voice' can be heard and heeded. Interest in developmental psychology (Erikson[6]), stages of faith (Fowler[7]), education (Piaget) and inter-relationships (Sullivan) predominate.

6. See III:13.
7. See V:25.

In this model there is a recognized tension between the power of good and the power of evil, and some uncertainty as to which might win out at any given time (both in the believer's heart and in world events). The story of Jesus dramatizes this tension, the best example being the temptation in the wilderness. Death is seen as interruptive of our active participation in the process of salvation history. After death there is the expectation that we might become part of a larger community (the communion of saints). Old Testament biblical theology is very influential, with the Exodus as a primary referential point. The prophet Hosea and the story of the Prodigal Son are two particularly poignant examples of God's constant wooing of us, while Hebrews 11 paints large the canvas of faithful people through the ages. (One student commented that if God can be seen as a Policeman in the first framework and us a kind of Emergency Medic in the second, then in this model God is certainly a tireless Negotiator and Lover).

Framework No. 4: The Completion of Creation
This framework reflects a radically wholistic outlook in which God and humanity, good and evil, suffering and joy are intrinsically interconnected one with the other. There is a synchronicity between the human and divine; the one mirrors the other; each weaves a tapestry which is the other. This is a non-hierarchial framework in which the radical potential exists for God to be as affected by us as we are by Him/Her. The need for the incarnation (Framework No. 2) is superseded by the presence of an 'I Am' which means 'we are'. Though evil and sin are powerful, the positive thrust of one-ness between God and creation is more powerful. In fact, because good and evil exist within creation *and* within God, they are both part of the natural ebb and flow of creation. Likewise, death is a part of life and accepted as such. 'From dust to dust' is an affirmation of basic order and therefore an expression of praise – not a sign of defeat. The creation, though filled with unknowns, is nevertheless trustworthy even though we may not necessarily be able to see all the *why's* and *wherefore's* ourselves. God is pre-eminently Creator in this model, and humanity is His/Her highest creative act and, therefore, blessed. Ecological concerns are in the forefront, for to save our creation is to save ourselves. We are all connected with one another so that family and group therapy, as well as general systems theory, are appealing modalities in the psychotherapeutic realm.

112

Whereas being in relationship was important in Framework No. 3, in this framework participation and responsibility are key concepts. Coming into one's full being, one's full potential, is the task of a faithful person, and Jesus (along with other prophets within other world religions) is a primary example. Pastoral care involves empowering people, affirming and blessing their personhood as unique, and praising God together for the gift of creation. There is faith here and in the natural order, that life's processes will carry us towards growth and light if we can but participate fully, and not be thrown by the inevitable ambiguities and uncertainties which will crop up. The story of Noah captures the optimism of this point of view. And the Book of Revelation points toward the way things are (nearing completion) and the way they will be finally (complete). Interest in eschatology (a 'hope against hope' *à la* Moltmann) is a subject for theological exploration, but only as a subtheme to the overall thrust of wholeness, participation, synchronicity and celebration.

Implications

. . .In discussions with students it also became apparent that we all move back and forth between these different frameworks depending on the degree of hopefulness, 'goodness' and self-confidence we feel on any given day. This is also true of our patients. Just as we tend to regress psychologically when faced with crisis or tragedy, so do we regress theologically. For example, a physically healthy person who lives comfortably within the ambiguities and the organic quality of Framework No. 4, when faced with unexpected crisis may move towards Framework No. 2, wanting to hear the more literal and specific story of Jesus the Christ as a means of 'holding on'. . . . .

Finally, one danger of outlining these frameworks in this way is the tendency to think of them as developmental in nature, so that a person moves 'back' towards No. 1 and 'forward' towards No. 4. Thinking in this way would imply a value judgement that some stages are more sophisticated and more 'healthy' than others. This is perhaps inevitable if the model is to be viewed in a linear, flat fashion. However, if it can be viewed multi-dimensionally, perhaps as a spiral with four inter-related strands varying in color and intensity with different energies and emphases flowing between and through all the strands causing the spiral to move and create ever-new patterns, then we are freer to explore the strengths and weaknesses of each framework within ourselves and others. The goal of such exploration is twofold: first, to recognize and claim our various theological 'parts'; and second, to decide what needs further development, what can be discarded, and what can be affirmed and delighted in . . .

V:27

Somewhat different from faith development or the faith framework is the theological world-view, which is summarized by the authors in the following extract. Their application of Tillich's ideas also permit me to mention this important theologian (see also p.94). Tillich, systematic theologian though he was, was constantly concerned with issues that inform pastoral care and counselling. Furthermore, because he moved in psychoanalytic circles, with Karen Horney, Erich Fromm, Abraham Maslow and many other important thinkers and writers, he writes in a language which the latter-day, theologically interested and psychologically-minded pastoral successor understands. References throughout this reader underline the importance of Tillich's influence, in such concepts as existential anxiety, etc. The reader who wishes to refer to this side of Tillich's work can read more in 'The Courage to Be' *(London, Fontana, 1962),* 'The Shaking of the Foundations' *(Harmondsworth, Penguin, 1962), or, as used in this article,* 'Dynamics of Faith' *(New York, Harper, 1957). In this extract I isolate the exegesis of some of Tillich's ideas and their application to pastoral care, omitting for reasons of space the three pastoral situations which preface the article, and to which the framework of the three world-views is applied. These can, of course, be found in the original. John Gleason, one of the authors, has since developed a four-World model; World D is set forth in ch. 15 of his book* 'Consciousness and the Ultimate' *(Abingdon Press, 1981).*

Three World-views [8]

Tillich's Gift

A. Writing in *Dynamics of Faith*, Paul Tillich sets forth in the chapter 'Symbols of Faith' three ways of relating to those symbols. It is the three ways of relating, the three world-views, the three spiritual worlds (World A, World B, and World C) that provide a theological framework for pastoral care. But first a word about definitions:

8. From W. E. Baldridge and J. J. Gleason, 'A Theological Framework for Pastoral Care' (*The Journal of Pastoral Care*, vol XXXII, no. 4, December 1978, pp. 232–8).

1. Faith is the state of being ultimately concerned.
2. Man's ultimate concern must be expressed symbolically, because symbolic language alone is able to express the ultimate.
3. A symbol points beyond itself while participating in that to which it points.
4. The myth is the combination of symbols of our ultimate concern.
5. It is the nature of myth that it uses material from our ordinary experience. It puts the stories of the gods into the framework of time and space although it belongs to the nature of the ultimate to be beyond time and space.

B. The first way of relating to the symbols of faith, World A, is what Tillich calls the natural stage of literalism. It is natural because it is the first stage of development and is found universally in primitive cultures as well as in childhood. It is literal because persons in World A make no distinction between the mythical and the literal. Symbols are understood in their immediate meaning and their character to point beyond themselves is not present.

In World A, the natural stage of literalism, there are no symbols, no myths. For example, creation is taken as an act that can be dated historically within seven 24-hour days. Spiritually speaking, a World A person is preconscious, feeling safe and certain. Tillich holds that 'This stage has a full right of its own and should not be disturbed, either in individuals or in groups, up to the moment when man's questioning mind breaks the natural acceptance of the mythological visions as literal'.

If, however, the natural stage of literalism, World A, becomes inadequate for the individual's level of questioning, Tillich believes that the person can move to either of two other ways of relating to symbols. Our own belief is that the three ways are developmental stages and that a definite sequence is followed, although some may move through the second stage, World B, very rapidly and many will never move beyond it.

C. The second way of relating to the symbols of faith, World B, Tillich has called the second stage of literalism or conscious literalism. When a literal understanding of symbol and myth is confronted by what can be verified through observation and experiment in such a way as to cast doubt upon that concreteness, one is thrust into World B. If the newly arrived World B person cannot or will not take on the anxiety of uncertainty that is a part of relating to symbols as symbols, that is, in a non-literal manner, the awareness of the questions and their inherent problems remains but it is half consciously, half unconsciously repressed. 'The tool of repression is usually an acknowledged authority with sacred qualities like the Church or the Bible, to which one owes unconditional surrender.'

The person who had no problem accepting creation as an act that took place in the course of a week may now experience a profound sense of anxiety when faced with the geological evidence that conflicts with a literal interpretation of the creation accounts. At the conscious stage of literalism, in World B, the anxiety is handled by receiving an answer from the sacred authority that allows the creation accounts to again be accepted literally. Any remaining anxiety is repressed.

This stage, like the first, is 'still justifiable, if the questioning power is very weak and can easily be answered'. But if the questions persist, grow more intense, or the answers provided by authority do not satisfy, or, as Tillich puts it, ' . . . a mature mind is broken in its personal center by political or psychological methods, split in his unity, and hurt in his integrity. . . .', conscious literalism is unjustifiable.

D. Tillich's alternative to conscious literalism and what we see as a third developmental stage, World C, is what he calls broken myth. Broken myth (or symbol) is a myth (or symbol) 'which is understood as a myth (or symbol) but is not removed or replaced'. To see a myth as a myth or symbol as a symbol is to recognize it as something pointing beyond itself while participating in that to which it points.

The reason a myth or symbol is not removed or replaced is because nothing else can take its place. Nothing else 'points beyond itself . . . participates in that to which it points . . . opens up levels of reality which otherwise are closed . . . unlocks dimensions and elements of our soul which correspond to the dimensions and elements of reality (opened by myth or symbol) . . . and grow(s) out of the individual or collective unconscious'. Nothing but a myth or symbol is able to express the ultimate.

An individual operating in World C retains the language of myth, the anthropomorphic image, the historical setting, because without them he or she has no language at all with which to speak about ultimate concern. A World C person breaks the code and gets the message. Although the code is not the message, the World C resident recognizes that without the code the message cannot be received. One still speaks of the second day of creation, for example, because the myth conveys something about the ultimate that only myth can do, but there is no problem when mythical truth encounters geological fact. Myth addresses the nature of the ultimate while geology attends to that which is less than ultimate, namely, the age of the earth.

That is not to say that one who replaces the unbroken myth of literalism with the broken myth is without problems. It is the World A person, operating within the security of natural literalism, who has no problems (or at least recognizes no problems) and thus has no anxiety; he or she is spiritually unconscious. The World B individual has the problem that in the second stage of literalism the system of repression must constantly be reinforced and fed by unconditional surrender to the authority. Conflicting authority cannot be recognized, much less tolerated. If the repression works well enough, the semi-conscious literalist again feels certain.

The World C problem, that caused by the break in literal understanding of myth, is a constant uncertainty which cannot be relieved by the magic of natural literalism or the sacred authority of conscious literalism. World C uncertainty can be answered only with faith and courage. Although faith and courage conquer uncertainty (doubt), they cannot 'eliminate it. 'Courage does not deny that there is doubt, but it takes the doubt into itself as an expression of its own finitude and affirms the content of an ultimate concern. Courage does not need the safety of an unquestionable conviction. It includes the risk without which no creative life is possible.'

Discussion

A. This theological framework for pastoral care is open to the just criticism of any model: oversimplification. In reality there is no pure World A, B, or C person. Remnants of A abound in World B and of A and B in World C. Even if it were possible to be pure World C, we would not wish it. The vestiges of the first two stages in the World C minister are the bases of genuine contact and empathy regarding someone in either the natural or the conscious state of literalism. Pastoral care in this mode is more than simply allowing persons to be where they are. If where they are meets their needs sufficiently, we can affirm them and their world-view out of our own experience that their way of relating to symbols once met all of our needs and continues to remain meaningful to us. We try to meet people where they are, but that is far from saying that we descend to where they are.

B. One might conclude that within this framework pastoral care is primarily a matter of maintenance; that there is no situation in which initiative or movement is appropriate. Not so. Pastoral care often takes the form of assisting persons to alter their understanding of symbols, and, through symbols, their relationship with the ultimate. The foundational conditions are that in some way the person must first signal for help, and that we must, in turn, respect that individual's personhood. On occasion we encounter a person at the threshold of moving from World A to B or from B to C, but these cases are relatively few. Our research indicates that the minister most frequently deals with a person in a World B context and that what is asked is that the minister help discover a more adequate World B way of relating to symbols of faith. Someone may have a concrete, anthropomorphic concept of God as angry, vindictive judge; movement could be toward a more loving, forgiving father-God concept.

C. We have shared here a theological conceptualization of what we are doing as pastoral care-givers. We believe this framework allows the minister to respond to a wide diversity of needs, all in good conscience (especially in relation to the exercise of pastoral authority).

One final comment: The pastoral care movement has been very successful in identifying and transmitting the tools of pastoral care-giving. However, these tools are held in common with all the helping professions, with the obvious exceptions such as the sacraments. Thus our role and identity cannot be fully defined by a job description alone. Through this theological framework pastors can more easily claim primary identity as those who deal with people in their relationship to what is ultimate in their lives, and who do so at the point of the use of the symbols of faith.

V:28

It is difficult to know how best to describe Frank Lake's work. British pastoral counselling owes him an enormous debt, for helping to put the discipline firmly on the map in the development of the clinical theology seminars. Many of today's more senior pastors received their first insights into this field through Lake and his tutors.[9] *Lake also provided in his person a link with the*

9. The Clinical Theology Association, following Lake's death, has undergone a type of rebirth (though not, I think, by using the primal methods which so enamoured Lake at the time of his death!). It has gone back to first principles and offers a new programme of seminars.

*international movement for pastoral care and counselling, known
and respected as he was in different continents.*

*His writing is an almost inextricable mixture of moments of pure
genius, and tedious terminology. Infatuated himself by often untried
ideas, or by the latest therapeutic fashion, especially when it
appeared to link clinical insights with theology, Lake moved too
rapidly into integrating his enthusiasms into his practice. At the
same time he was not afraid to leave behind that which had outlived
its usefulness (such as his early experimenting with LSD). His
'Clinical Theology' remains largely unread, if at one time it was
frequently referred to. An abridged version of 'the tome' may re-
awaken interest in the more permanently valuable parts of Lake's
writing.*[10] *'Tight Corners in Pastoral Counselling' is also an
abridgement, to one-third of the size of the original papers sent to
his publisher. It is from that book, now out of print, that I take a
few pages – from the chapter called 'Infatuation and the Divine'.
The chapter shows Lake at his startling best, jolting the reader
into an awareness which is somewhat like the actual situation he
describes. Substitute ideological passion for sexual passion, and
perhaps the passage is also a fitting tribute to a man whom the
eventual history of pastoral care and counselling in our time has
still to assess.*

Infatuation and the Divine [11]

Yet there are times when the sudden heat of a devouring passion
in the form of a bolt-from-the-blue infatuation, calling a person
to throw up all and follow 'the star', comes as a welcome shaking
of sadly inadequate foundations. Some people's lives have had
their foundations laid in the rubbish dump of cultural left-overs
and the family throw-outs for several generations. They have
never penetrated down to the solid ground even of their own
perception of reality or to genuine feelings of their own about
life.

There are those whose only concern is that this man or woman
get back into line. He or she must cool off this unaccustomed
ardour, must recognize that the mediocrity into which marital life
settles down in middle-class society is the most that can be
expected of it. Romance is for romantic novels or the television.

10. M. Yeomans (ed.), *Clinical Theology* (London, Darton Longman and Todd,
1986).
11. From F. Lake, *Tight Corners in Pastoral Counselling* (London, Darton
Longman and Todd, 1981), pp. 166–71, used by permission of the publishers.

It is to be indulged in only vicariously, in fantasies of identification with the hero and the heroine. Then go to bed with your wife or husband, and imagine both of you as other than you are.

A counsellor, especially if he or she is to be relied upon to take a safe, churchy line, has, in the view of such people, only one task: to prick the bubble and deflate this balloon. If, by tomorrow, this hot passion of a heart-sick lover can become, by skilled counselling, as cold as if it had never been, so much the better. If he returns to the safe, tepid waters of a dull, domestic co-existence, the counsellor will have done a good job. I have often been very aware of these expectations surrounding me.

But then some awkward texts come to mind, inviting you to consider this case in their strangely blinding light. There are the words of the Son of man in the Revelation to St John. They come from the radiant figure 'from [whose] mouth issued a sharp two-edged sword, and his face was like the sun shining in full strength' (Rev. 1:16 R.S.V.). They are the words to the Church in Laodicea:

> The words of the Amen, the faithful and true witness, the beginning of God's creation. 'I know your works: you are neither cold nor hot. Would that you were cold or hot! So, because you are lukewarm, and neither cold nor hot, I will spew you out of my mouth. For you say, I am rich, I have prospered, and I need nothing; not knowing that you are wretched, pitiable, poor, blind, and naked. Therefore I counsel you to buy from me gold refined by fire. (Rev. 3:14–18 R.S.V.)

The lukewarmness of the Laodiceans, which nauseates God, is a basic ingredient of that denial of passion which leads to a pseudo-servility in which those who are embedded in it feel smug and self-satisfied. Something with the violence of passion has to come along to shake them out of this blindness. With the scales removed they can have eyes to see that, under God, the destiny of man is an election to an unending glory, an expanding lover-beloved relationship. The pressuring culture of which he is a compliant part is not greater, or more long lasting than he is. He will outlive it. But he must begin, now, to live outside it, or the new road to life is never begun.

Suppose I am in the presence of a man who is still in a fiery furnace, burnt up with longing for his lady-love. This is a 'divine' invasion. Let us not quarrel here about the difference between the theological and the popular use of 'divine' as an adjective. A certain kind of morality strives to dub this whole excursion into passion as 'godlessness'. Our text indicates a greater godlessness in a contented self-cosseting mentality, moulded by mediocrity. The counsellor's task is to perceive the moment or fragment of truth in this grand illusion. Its value is not in pursuing it for itself. That would be further delusion. Its value is in its ability to broaden and deepen greatly the experiential dimensions of a personality. It is in its power to break up monotony and arouse expectations of something better, something more alive, joyful, vivacious, exciting and glorious, that we come to value it in the divine economy.

Anything that can begin the process of disrupting a deadly drift through life, plodding and snoozing, complying and preening oneself by turns, is a potential Godsend. One of the cardinal principles of Christian pastoral counselling is that 'everything is usable'. With the gold of Christ's fiery trial brought alongside him, our infatuated man may begin to purchase, from the shared experience, that 'gold refined by fire' which the two-edged sword-tongued Son of man counsels here. It is our task to make clear that this transformation is possible, and how it is possible.

This person has never before noticed the glory of God in his handiwork, the glory of a man made in his image, or of a woman bearing a reflection of his radiance. God is not directly present in his handiwork. If our closed-in lives are broken up to see, not only the wonder of the infinitely attractive other person, but also the even greater compelling authority of the ethical to restrain our chasing after it, we enter a whole new world; but God is still not directly present to us. . . .

Now, in this unruly falling-in-love, [this man] has had an overwhelming experience that has lifted him out of the rut. Within himself he is at least sure of something, by the self-evident truth of his own strong, and for the first time indisputable, subjective feelings. He is taken over by them, lifted by the scruff of the neck, one might say, out of himself, and out of the social matrix to which he had looked slavishly for esteem in return for compliance. This is too precious a moment not to be seized upon in the service of a truth greater than itself.

So the first obstacle to be overcome in counselling is likely to be that of the 'transference' expectation. Our man will expect to hear from the counsellor the voice of the 'Parent', condemning, deprecating, warning, with nothing good to say about the whole episode. His defences will be up to defend it. Before he has wakened up to the fact that we are speaking in an Adult way to his Adult, he is likely to mistake our positive evaluation of his experience, and the lack of a note of condemnation in our voice, as our siding with the Child in its enthusiasm for this discovery of unimagined glory. He may take it that we approve heartily of his relationship with this 'direct' representative of immortal Love itself. But our empathy with the Child's breakthrough into archetypal joys is not the same as a compliant sympathy such as would totally share his exaltation and support the resolution to carry it through. Somehow, we must communicate that difference. Eventually, if a sound Adult-to-Adult relationship can be made, the work will have some real chance of success. We are able then to appeal from Philip 'drunk' to Philip 'sober', without going by way of Philip 'bad'. . . .

This citizen and father had not only never discovered the glory of God in his handiwork, he had, by the same token, passed through life 'without ever having received any impression of the infinitude of the ethical'.[12] He has now broken out of the social shell or cultural cocoon. He is snatched up into an all-engrossing passion that stretches him into dimensions of being and commitment that threaten all the conventional ethics of his quite correct upbringing. 'Therefore shall a man leave his father and mother and cleave to his wife' (Matt. 19:5). His old marriage had been such a family affair, with the parents on both sides so pleased to see them safely wed. All that talk about 'leaving and cleaving' seemed overdramatic at the time, and just not applicable. But now he feels, in the deepest fibre of his nature, aglow with the kind of adoration and longing that for the first time makes sense of the drama of leaving and cleaving. He passionately desires to leave his wife, and to cleave – elsewhere.

He has not explored this road far as 'a Christian' before he collides with the Word of Christ about adultery, even to the extent of looking 'on a woman to lust after her' (Matt. 5:28 A.V.). For the first time in his life, whichever way he ultimately decides to go, he has 'received an impression of the infinitude of the ethical'.

The counsellor may meet the woman in question or see her photograph. She usually has youth on her side. She still enjoys all that age has still to take away from her in looks. Beyond that, the cooler eye of the observer often senses that the beauty the love-sick man worships is in his own eye as the beholder. Most of what delights him as he looks at her is derived from his own inner endowment, projected upon her. His own blessed and wholly adorable primal or archetypal image of the ideal feminine figure has, by some quirk of fortune or fate, fastened upon her. He thinks, indeed he is totally convinced that it all belongs to her, and that to lose her is to lose all. In fact, he could withdraw these projections without loss to himself. He would only be taking back

12. Quotation from Kierkegaard, used earlier in this chapter.

his own. But to convince a man or a woman of that fact is never easy. Indeed, to make the attempt directly is to forget all that one has learnt in personal experience about the force and finality of projection, particularly when support from ordinary sources has been withdrawn from the ego. Self-criticism weakens, defensiveness begins.

If, at times, projection seems to account for most of the fixation, at others one is aghast at the genuine contrast between a wife who has become sharp, bitter and shrewish, and a lovely woman who genuinely loves this married man, who flowers in her presence. Aghast, because the pastoral counsellor has no authority to dispense with the word of Christ who, in the final judgement, has the last word. Christ's sovereign and final word is in the forgiveness of sins, but there is a fearful responsibility in becoming an accessory to making a decision to sin. Though in this chapter I have been principally concerned with projection and fixation, there is another set of tight corners, where reality factors in the marriage make their own contribution.

V:29

The question posed in this part, the relationship of the pastoral counsellor's faith to her or his practice, is a similar one to that addressed by Quentin Hand in the next extract. He writes that 'the attempt to explain one's faith is the "doing of theology" '. I do not happen to agree with all that Hand does in the case example he gives; nor would he expect me too, because he recognizes that various therapists would react differently to Ellen's question about his certainty of God's existence. At the same time I welcome the willingness to reflect theologically upon his practice, and for this reason include much of his article. Its total length has meant the omission of a second incident, which he says would not have occurred with a secular psychotherapist; and I have to omit too the outcome of Ellen's pastoral counselling. Sufficient is included to encourage the pastoral counsellor to consider the possibility of thinking theologically about practice (and when appropriate invite the client to do the same), even though, as Hand himself concludes, this is not to advocate that all must share the same theological interpretation.

'Doing' Theology in Pastoral Counselling [13]

My thesis is

> Pastoral counseling is the practice of theology by a minister in his or her interaction with one or more persons in the quest for wholeness of relationship with God, world and others, and in the quest for the integrity of the persons involved.

Theology is the reasoned statement of the meanings which are implicit and explicit in faith. These are meanings about God, about the world, about humans, and about the relationships among God and world and humans. Theology is the conceptual formulation of one's faith. . . .

The attempt to explain one's faith is the 'doing' of theology. It is the active reflection upon one's own experience in order to state meanings in contemporary thought forms. . . .

Among the committed, 'doing' theology leads to new depths of understanding of faith. It expands the areas of life in which faith guides decision making. Hence, 'doing' theology means new expressions of doctrine and new sensitivity to social justice. . . .

The practice of theology is the use of one's own behavior to aid another in developing faith and in making a faith commitment. The practice of theology is the use of language or of actions to share one's own faith in ways that others can understand and can accept. It may require sharing meaning in symbolic or in elementary form in order for the other to receive it. . . .

In my experience, few seekers ask for help in theological terms. They name specific tensions, such as a troubled marriage, or depression, or inability to keep friends, as the cause of coming to the minister. Since they have asked a pastoral counselor for help, the initial evaluation of their need must be made by the minister. The words used to tell the seeker how the pastoral counselor understands him or her will be chosen to fit that person. But the diagnosis made by a pastoral counselor will be theological.

The basic theological categories for understanding the seeker will be the doctrines of personhood or anthropology, of creation, and of sin. I am considering primarily the doctrine of sin as a means of understanding a person. I am aware of at least three types of definitions of sin; they are first, violation of ritual restrictions; second, violation of law or moral code; and third, violation of one's potential, or failure to achieve the mark. All of these rest

13. From Q. L. Hand, 'Pastoral Counseling as Theological Practice' (*The Journal of Pastoral Care*, vol. XXXII, no. 2, June 1978, pp. 100–10).

upon a sense of an obligation that has not been kept. All of them are individualistic.

My definition of sin does not fit into any one of these categories. For me,

> *Sin* is a theological construct describing that quality of a relationship between two or more persons (one of whom may be God) which interferes with the harmonious and reciprocal interaction of each to the other, of each to the social and physical world, and of each within the parts of one's own organism.

This definition sees the locus of sin in the relationship rather than in a person . . .

Now let us relate this definition to pastoral counseling experience. In 1972 I was part-time Minister of Counseling in an Atlanta church. Ellen Ross asked for an appointment. She had a skin rash, which a dermatologist had been treating for three years without improvement. . . .

Ellen was aware of tensions with three persons. Her differences with Bob, her husband, were expressed in her reluctance to have sexual intercourse and in doing housework poorly; Ellen referred to herself as a lazy housekeeper. Both of them had trouble in managing money, as they tended to spend freely. Ellen's mother-in-law, Susie, was a lonely widow who visited her husband's grave every week and wanted Bob, her only child, to fill the void in her life. Ellen stifled her resentment of her mother-in-law, and it was several months into our counseling relationship before she expressed it to me. Also, Ellen had difficulty parenting Deborah, the second child; Ellen could neither love her freely nor discipline her. She said about Deborah, 'She is too much like me'. . . .

Sin, as I define it, is present in Ellen's life in several dimensions. Ellen's relationship with her husband was neither harmonious nor reciprocal. He would wash the dishes in anger and scold her for allowing them to accumulate. Ellen saw his sexual desire as wanting service rather than expressing love for her. She felt herself a housekeeper, and she did not sustain a partner and mate relationship with Bob. Ellen was threatened by Bob's mother, Susie, and by Susie's desire for Bob's primary attention. Ellen tried to do what her mother-in-law asked in order to keep peace, but she did so resentfully. Ellen and Susie were enemies. Ellen saw herself in her own daughter, so Ellen did not know Deborah. Ellen was responding to her projection, and she had a limited relationship to Deborah. Sin, as a theological understanding of relationships, was present in these major ties of mate, parent and child in Ellen's life.

But use of the category of sin alone is inadequate. God's grace is evident in the loving parents Ellen had, in the meaningful religious life she had in adolescent and adult years, in her closeness to her deceased father-in-law, and in the conscientious dermatologist who treated her eczema. God's call to participation in a community was evident in the quality of Ellen's nuclear family as a child, in her extended family as an adult, and in her numerous friendships. God's judgment is apparent in Ellen's self-evaluation as poor housekeeper and in the skin rash.

If my theological practice stopped at this point of diagnosis, it would not make a difference to Ellen. I did not use these words in talking to Ellen at that time. These were for my understanding then and for your understanding now. Since a pastoral counseling relationship is to contribute to the need of the seeker, evaluation or diagnosis must be followed by prescription.

I hold that the goal of pastoral counseling as theological practice is the redemption of the seeker. A minister who specializes in counseling is using a specific communication mode to express and to advance the faith. A person seeking help from a minister knows the minister represents God in a special way. However the seeker verbalizes the desired result, a wish for contact with God is implied. And I, as pastoral counselor, see the covenant relationship of the person with God and community as the ultimate goal of pastoral counseling. The goal of pastoral counseling is the redemption of the seeker.

The definition of redemption which I hold is:

Redemption is a theological construct describing that quality of a relationship between two or more persons (one of whom may be God) which contributes to the developing and sustaining of commitment and mutual reciprocity of each to the other, of each to the social and physical world, and of each within the parts of his or her own organism in order to effect love and wholeness for each and to extend love and wholeness as widely as possible beyond the immediate relationship.

It was my specific goal with Ellen to aid her in forming redemptive relationships with Bob, with her mother-in-law Susie, and with Deborah. I hoped she would know God in a new way, with a more mature commitment. It was my conviction that her skin rash, as an expression of God's judgment, would disappear as her sinful separation was acknowledged and forgiven.

Theological practice of counseling means that Ellen's relationship to me as minister is where doctrines will become practiced and effective. As sin is recognized and judged and forgiven in the counseling relationship, the separation/alienation will be reduced. And this will contribute to recognition and judgment and pardon in other relationships also. The consequences of change reach beyond the immediate counseling relationship. As Ellen and I move from a relationship of two sinners using one another for self-centered purposes to a relationship of two redeemed persons, then Ellen will be more able to be a loving mate to Bob, an understanding daughter-in-law to Susie, and a trustworthy mother to Deborah.

To this counseling relationship, I bring my own covenant with God and church, my understanding of human growth and limits, and my awareness that I am both representative of God to Ellen and also sinner with God in my own person. I have a responsibility to understand and to contribute to our work which Ellen does not have. She seeks help; I am to practice theology, to make theology life and blood and understanding in my body and words and actions. I am to practice theology, to make Gospel alive, to be Incarnation and judgment and grace and pardon and invitation to commitment to Ellen as she asks for help.

This statement needs illustration. In our nineteenth session I asked how the skin rash was. Ellen told me it was continuing. Then she told of reading articles in *Guideposts* on the reality of God. She asked if I were certain God existed.

My reply was to relate an experience I had had several years previously. I had been very lonely and homesick. Late at night I knelt praying in the college chapel. I received a certainty of God's presence, sensed as a physical nearness, which obliterated my homesickness. That certainty has never left me. Ellen thanked me for telling her and left. In the following sessions she began open expression of her anger, which had been repressed in the first eighteen sessions we had.

I understand her request to have been testing my trustworthiness. Her need had been expressed initially in seeking help. Her sinful defence against both closeness and pain was evident in the obedient quality of her talking in the first eighteen sessions. But now she was questioning God's availability, and this was asking about my availability as God's representative. . . .

My reply was theological practice. I wanted to be loving and trustworthy as God's representative. I wanted to be God-with-humans in sharing her sin. I wanted to be grace-full, the expression of grace, in meeting her challenge helpfully. In telling my own loneliness I shared her sense of isolation and identified with it. In

127

telling my own efforts and my prayer, I acknowledged her search for help as acceptable and as understood. In affirming that God came to me I embodied the eschatological promise that God would come to her. But *also*, I was telling her that God was present in that moment of the counseling session in me. Hence, God was, *in me*, responding to her question by the divine presence then and there!

My reply gave more personal involvement than some theories of counseling approve. My reply reduced Ellen's anxiety, and some theories would not have reduced anxieties at this point. But my intention was her redemption. And the timing of grace rather than judgment, of immanence rather than transcendence, was the issue. This was theological practice rather than healing a psychosomatic condition.

Part VI

The Critique of Pastoral Counselling

Publishers' lists bear witness to the vogue that exists for pastoral as well as other forms of counselling, and for informing pastoral care through counselling skills and models. Merely to foster uncritical interest in pastoral care and counselling would be to promote that type of idealization, idolization, or inauthentic defence against the anxieties of pastoral ministry that pastoral counselling itself tries to interpret. In this last part, I have therefore chosen representative arguments against the fashion for pastoral counselling and individualistic pastoral care, as well as against the excessive preoccupation with self, which the psychological invasion of faith and theology may be in danger of creating.

VI:30

Dr R. A. ('Bob') Lambourne was a psychiatrist and pastoral theologian for whom those who worked or studied with him have immense respect. He lectured in Pastoral Studies at the University of Birmingham from 1964 until his premature death in 1972. Lambourne's papers exercised a critical faculty, particularly about the then developments in pastoral counselling in Britain (when a national organization was first under discussion), which cost him much to put into print, perhaps even hastening his death. Clearly, as the next extract shows, he did not wish to hurt or offend; yet he passionately saw the dangers present on the paths pastoral counselling appeared to be taking. This paper, written in 1969, is only one of those in which he raises vital objections. It is a tightly argued essay, of which less than half can be included here.[1] Lambourne is more critical of Rogerian and other humanistic therapies than he is of Freudian analysis, for the reasons stated in the article. Presumably 'ego-psychology', which he judges more severely, refers to the

1. Others include 'Objections to a National Pastoral Organisation' (*Contact* 35 and *Explorations in Health and Salvation*) and 'Personal Reformation and Political Formation in Pastoral Care' (*Contact* 44 and *Explorations in Health and Salvation*).

humanistic version of this; and not to Freudian ego-psychology as it has developed in Britain and America, since post-Freudians of this type, in turning their attention to ego-development and ego-defences, have not abandoned their interest in the id (the instinctual/impulsive part of the conscious and unconscious self). The other technical terms which may need explanation are Lambourne's coined phrases 'egoism–à-deux' or 'narcissism-à-deux': these are adapted from the phrase 'folie-à-deux' which describes a phenomenon whereby two people interpenetrate each other in thought or action, and support each other in their 'folly', without any apparent ability to step back and recognize their own separateness, or their own and the other's irrationality.

Counselling for Narcissus or Counselling for Christ? [2]

Introduction

This paper is a harsh attack on pastoral counselling as the writer believes it to be widely taught and practised at present. This pastoral counselling shows little sign, either by definition or practice, of a living relationship with the fellowship of the Church as corporately understood. . . .

However, it must be stated emphatically, that if in the first pages it appears that the attack is against psychotherapy or counselling *per se* then it is unfortunate for the opposite is the writer's intention. He believes that true pastoral counselling ought to be more central and more important to the Church than it is at present. However, this cannot be the case until pastoral counselling is rediscovered for what it is: namely, the Church growing towards perfection (towards maturity) as, taught of God, it learns in the service of God and neighbour what it must do to be saved. This process is centred on responsible acts, and is a learning and a doing of Christian behavioural ethics by the fellowship (*koinonia*). The knowledge of what to do and the power to do it, takes the shape of a responsible act. Both knowledge and power to act are experienced by the two or three or more as *given*, as pure grace, and naturally this is shown by thankful prayer. Such pastoral counselling ceases to be a dubious activity on the margins of the Church, it becomes its centre and its strengh rather than weakening it. . . .

How shall we describe pastoral counselling in an orderly way

2. From R. A. Lambourne, (ed. M. Wilson), *Explorations in Health and Salvation* (University of Birmingham Institute for the Study of Worship and Religious Architecture, 1983), pp. 135–61

without offering a final definition? Let us say that pastoral counselling receives its character from that of which it is a part, namely, the Christian fellowship of two or more deciding what they must do together to be the Church in the world. It is not, it will be noted, concerned with individual salvation. It is not a pietistic methodism. It is not for man, but for God for man. . . . Where the Church is, pastoral counselling is, and vice versa. If one is totally absent then the other is absent.

But pastoral counselling at the moment doesn't look much like this because:

1. It does not take either subjective or objective 'facts' sufficiently seriously;
2. It does not treat scripture expectantly with subjective and objective sensitivity;
3. It is individualistic and does not regard itself as the *koinonia* of two or three;
4. It does not take theology or philosophy seriously;
5. It does not experience the insightful decision and power to act as grace;
6. It does not voice that experience of grace by thanksgiving.

The end result is that pastoral counselling is a heretical movement. It weakens the Church and has within it the seeds of a complete schism. Those who separate themselves from the Church and set up pastoral counselling offices are merely carrying things to a logical conclusion. Careful plans for repentance and renewal of pastoral counselling within the Church must therefore be made immediately.

Main argument
What is it that holds 'pastoral' and 'counselling' together, so that one can speak of 'pastoral counselling' or of being a 'pastoral counsellor'? It is certainly not united by a common body of knowledge derived from the behavioural sciences, a kind of technical anthropological dogmatics. The agreed 'facts' are few. If anything, the 'factual' element in counselling is divisive since the supposed facts are assembled into different bundles of knowledge which are almost as diverse as the numbers of counsellors. . . . This multiplication of schools has been especially apparent in the United States of America as with religious sectarianism. . . .

Faced with the above situation many apologists of counselling seem to be diverting attention from the 'factual basis' of the authority and efficacy of counselling, and thereby to play down how little we know in the way of 'facts'. Previously psychotherapy and counselling were alleged to be authoritative and efficacious (in contrast to traditional religious methods) because they were based upon a clinical method and upon clinical facts which did not involve ethical value judgements. But now they are claimed to be authoritative and efficacious because of some consistent 'attitude' embodied in the technique, such as 'unconditional acceptance', 'unconditional commitment' or 'open-ness to experience'. . . .

When one looks at counsellors themselves and those who are happy to call themselves successful clients, a certain similarity is noticeable about their value systems. . . . They have been persuaded towards the ethical humanism characteristic of western democratic liberalism. (The recent new radicalism which is distrustful of liberalism has little good to say for psychotherapy and counselling.) . . .

Counselling, then, is an ethical process – and not just in the weak sense that there are ethical matters involved in everything to do with human beings (as for example, surgery). . . .

. . . sociological research into counsellors, counselling and allied work will produce data likely to have the same chastening effect as the sociology of religion has had on religion. Demonstrations of high correlation between certain political opinions, a certain type of counselling experience, and attitudes to matters like racial segregation, extramarital intercourse and child-rearing, will show how much counselling affiliation is ideological affiliation, just as it has done in the field of religion. . . .

At this point it must be made clear that the word 'ethics' is not being used as a synonym for the prescription of precise rules about what is invariably right and wrong in stereotyped situations. Indeed, a tendency to move towards a psychological ethical legalism will later be deplored. No, ethics is being used to designate the foundations and principles of human behaviour. . . .

The proper task of pastoral counselling should have been twofold. *First*, to concentrate on adapting the techniques to the distinctive patterns of church life and to the work of the Minister of religion, so that prayer, bible reading, sacraments and preaching took the place of the couch. *Second*, to let the ideologies feel not only the influence of those changed circumstances but also the analysis of theology and philosophy. Sadly, what happened was that pastoral counselling swallowed the whole job lot, and so no distinctive pastoral counselling has emerged. Indeed as the years have passed pastoral counselling has emptied life of Christian symbols and replaced them with psycho-therapeutic ones, so that the task has become harder. Even worse, the tendency has been in some psychotherapeutic circles and some pastoral

132

counselling ones to get rid of the baby and leave the bath water. That is, they have let go of the rigorous clinical method (leading to a humble, penultimate diagnosis, a particular ethical formation for one person) and concentrated on a mixture of technique and ideologies. This only looks too much like the old discredited ways of Christian pastoralia. . . .

Having said such hard things against so much of present psychotherapy and secular counselling, and the pastoral counselling influenced by them, the question arises about the future relation between them, and between them and the Church. . . . There could be a good case for saying 'No, we must separate ourselves, come out from among the Canaanites; begin again though it means leaving behind many good things; start with two or three Christian brothers gathered together under God in the congregation, and work out a new pastoral counselling which is just one specialized part of Christian liturgy'. However, this would cause separation and weakness when what we want is a reunion of pastoral counselling with the Church so that both may be stronger. So we will turn our 'No' into a 'No, maybe'. . . .

The strong 'No' is a 'No' to the shift from id-psychology to ego-psychology and on to the 'ego-divinization-à-deux' psychology which is rampant today. This 'No' to ego-psychology is based upon the assessment (to anticipate what is said later) that ego-psychology as it is current today, courts psychological disaster in the shape of narcissism. It also threatens a theological disaster, namely asserting that ego in relationship with ego is God. It means a 'No' therefore to Feuerbach and Fromm and their theological and psychological successors, and to all those who have anthropologized Christ by separating him from the transcendent Father who sent his only beloved son. But the 'maybe' of the 'No, maybe' is a qualified 'No' to Barth, and at the same time it is a qualified 'Yes' to secular counselling (provided it will stop reducing 'revelation' to the counsellor's experiences in therapy). This qualified 'Yes' to counselling and qualified 'No' to Barth is based upon a natural theology which asserts that in the Christian life redemption in Christ takes place in the world in which God gives himself to be grasped by man. . . .

The harsh judgement against ego-psychology may cause astonishment. Is not ego-psychology (unlike id-psychology) a good model for pastoral counselling since it is so much closer to the Christian idea of a free-at-the-centre person? No, not as it is conceived today. *Firstly*, because the very difference of id-psychology makes conversation between psychoanalysis and theology harder, and therefore less likely to slide into synchretism.

Secondly, and more important, because the radicality of the id-ego enmity kept Freud (in this respect as in many others) within the Judaeo-Christian myth, with its sense of the depth of the flaw in man. Here was retained a sense of something akin to the conviction of sin that Christ's love and perfection brings to man with the Good News. But the ego-psychology of today, often combined with a Zen Buddhism from which the sense of finitude has been removed, produces a sophisticated, confident, ego-divinization-in-relationship which knows neither sin nor salvation. Man, Pelagian man, knows of nothing from which he cannot deliver himself in relationship to another. He both determines what are his possibilities and grasps them.

The present situation is that most pastoral counselling has all but lost its belief in any other God than the I-Thou relationship as God: and it has all but lost its connection with the Church as the body within which pastoral counselling is done. . . . Thus unconditional(!) commitment and unconditional(!) acceptance has no need of any other sacrifice, and the lamb caught in the thicket is redundant. But it doesn't work. Sadly it leads to disillusionment and despair. Each of the two egos [i.e. counsellor and client – Ed.] has made an idol of the other, confused the idol with God, made the other an unbroken symbol, made an ultimate commitment to what is not ultimate.

Absolute commitment and absolute acceptance or openness are disasters psychologically and blasphemous theologically speaking. Psychologically they may be understood as total disalienation, a non-separation, an undifferentiated identity. Of this horror the incest taboo is a symbol, a flaming sword which bars the way to a narcissism-à-deux[3] which is death to the soul. Enlarged, narcissism-à-deux becomes community idolatry, and the error of individualism is replaced by the error of mass man, as egoism-à-deux changes into narcissism-à-deux. . . . Trinitarian Christology (by which we know that the Christ who is the other for me always transcends the other and me) resists the reduction of Christology to anthropology. It denies the possibility of two I's perfectly knowing each other, revealing each other, affirming each other, creating each other, being gods to each other – *except by grace given in weakness in Christ*, whereby we are strong, men come of age, more than conquerors. . . .

'This is incredible', some readers will say. The ideal human

---

3. For explanation of this term, see introduction to this extract.

being of depth psychologists like Fromm[4] is so Christian. Look at *The Art of Loving*: it is more clearly Christian than the gospels! Absolute acceptance, absolute commitment, and all under the law of love! (Ah, there's the rub – the *law* of love.) But *of course* it is like Christ, as the liberal humanist sees Christ. And it will become more so; for what is being done, patient by patient for our generation, is the process which Feuerbach advocated page by page in *The Essence of Christianity*. It is turning theology into anthropology, God into man. Soaked as he is in thousands of years of ethical monotheism, the therapist looks down the well and sees the divine man. So ego-psychology is the laboratory of the theology of atheism. That theology operates with a Christology which is an exact analogue of what the therapist does for the patient. He frees him to be free *like himself*! That means free to make others to be free to free others to be free like himself. Note the double meaning of 'free like himself'. Not just free, but free after my style of being free. So the *Imago Dei* becomes the Imago Freudiensis, Frommiensis or what have you. Certainly God made men to be gods, but like God. To be God like man is to break the first commandment. . . .

If pastoral counselling would return both to its disciplined methods and to the Church they could strengthen each other enormously. At present Christian worship and Christian theology, through not being tied closely enough to the facts of life, to the making of responsible decisions and to personal and political experiences, tend to lose their vitality. Pastoral counselling, because it is not tied to the Church gradually slips into foreign ideologies, and such meaningful symbols as it develops build up a separate mythology shared by a separated community of faith. The two brought together could bring life to each other. Therefore we must do as has been suggested, and change mistaken under-standings of both Church and pastoral counselling by a joint defi-nition of both, which does justice to the scriptural and traditional understanding of both Church and ethics. Thus we say that the pastoral counselling which is usually understood nowadays as the specialized activity of a professional person, will receive its character and authority from that pastoral counselling which is the *koinonia* of two or three together gathered in the Church to discover and to do such responsible acts in the service of God, the neighbour and each other as must be done; that they through God in Christ may be brought individually and corporately to mature perfection – may be saved. This does not confine the

4. See III:12.

koinonia to either the church building or the place where the ordained Minister is, but to where Christian brother meets Christian brother. This is the base and the definition. But this does not mean that the Church withdraws into itself to counsel itself: for the missionary structure of a congregation (which is a pastorally counselling community by definition) means that pastoral counselling sees its task as being set by the needs of the world. Moreover, whilst pastoral counselling is a function of the whole Church, this does not mean that within it many ministries may not be authorized, and of these the ministry of pastoral counselling may be one. But this does not mean that the members of *every* Christian group (as priests for one another) are not pastoral counsellors of one another.

VI:31

James Mathers, whose death occurred in 1986, was a colleague of Lambourne's at Birmingham. He said that his paper, part of which follows, cannot be read in ignorance of Lambourne's papers. He was too modest, because his writing stands in its own right; but the links between his ideas and Lambourne's are clear, as comparison with the former extract shows. Mathers writes a few years later, and is less anxious about counselling, but nonetheless develops Lambourne's concern that pastoral counselling must examine its background and context.

A Christian Counsellor's Perspective [5]

A Counselling Stance
We may distinguish here between the humanist and the Christian counsellor. The humanist may indeed offer forgiveness by his attitude of acceptance, but his attentive awareness is likely to stay focused on the person or persons he is counselling, and to omit the deepest level, of sensitivity to the word of God in the situation. At his best, he is likely to be the kind of counsellor who makes an idolatry of human relationships; who takes his love for his neighbour as ultimate but fails to leave room for the love of God. There are many such, and they may do admirable work within this limited context. But the Christian counsellor, similarly offering

5. From J. Mathers, 'How Far Does the Evangel Impinge Upon Counselling Practice?' (*Contact*, 57, 1977:2, pp. 2–11).

136

forgiveness, does not interpret this as his own contribution, but rather as that of his Master.

Humility and Vision
Thus there are three ways in which the Christian counsellor is called to a particular humility and self-abnegation. He is called to see his encounter with another person as one between equals, rather than between himself as strong and the other as weak. He is called to resist the temptation to use the power at his disposal to solve the other's problems. This is sometimes a function of pastoral care, of doing; but counselling is concerned with knowing, not doing. And third, he is called to realize that any benefit – to himself or the other – which emerges from the consultation is God's work rather than his own. Such humility and self-denial is hard to achieve and hard to bear. . . . Surely, to put aside our role as the dispensers of counsel, as those who possess skill and power, would be to leave ourselves naked and defenceless? Can the blind lead the blind? Will they not both fall into the pit? In fact, I suggest that the model of the blind leading the blind is a very appropriate image for counselling; and preferable to that of the Good Samaritan, which leaves unconsidered the important question of mutuality in loving and reciprocity in understanding. If two blind men fall into a pit, they can still support each other, and may yet find a way out. . . .

Wholeness
At all events, such a perspective has three practical implications. First, the Christian will be reminded that since what he is seeking is the kingdom of God and his righteousness, his holiness, his wholeness – he must always pay as much attention to wholes as he does to parts. It means that he sees the other not only as himself, but as a representative of his family, his work-group, his community. The counsellor will not only try to see Christ in the man before him, but will realize that Christ is also present in those to whom that man is related outside the counselling situation. And so he will be as ready to encounter them as to meet with him alone. Thus he will find the courage to tackle group counselling, to move into community, even though he knows that groups and communities will convict him of powerlessness in a way which the one-to-one relationship commonly hides from him. He can begin to see how a corporate understanding of health and holiness is the context which gives meaning to, and sets limits to the value of, one-to-one counselling.

The second implication of this perspective is that it makes clear

137

that it is the system of values which the Christian brings to counselling that carries healing and reconciling power rather than his technical skill. Without Christian values (whether they are called by this name or not) skills are no more than sounding brass or a tinkling cymbal. Technical ability is valuable in solving defined and limited problems. That is what it is for. But it is a fact of experience that, from a contextual or ecological viewpoint, the solution of one problem merely transfers the stresses and strains to a different location in time or space. . . . Problem solving is thus of only transient importance. But the counsellor's scale of values makes an enduring contribution, for better or worse, to the re-ordering of other people's experience: it alters the perspective from which problematic situations are seen, whether it makes them easier to deal with or not.

The third implication is more difficult. When we equip ourselves by learning skills and techniques, we tend to see ourselves as individually responsible for the way we employ them; and the notion of individual responsibility implies a degree of egocentricity. But as soon as we have learnt the discipline and humility proper in a soldier in Christ's army, we begin to see ourselves less as separate soldiers in his army, and rather as cells that form an integral part of his Body. . . . Our identities become Christocentric instead of egocentric. And within the constraints of love which this implies, we become paradoxically free to be as concerned with our own well-being as with that of others: you can love your neighbour as yourself, and love yourself as you do your neighbour. We come to see one another as more uniquely distinct selves even as we relinquish our view of one another as mutually independent.

VI:32

In Thornton's 'Theology and Pastoral Counseling'[6] *the importance of true* koinonia *appears again; although here he suggests, and is surely right, that the blame for pastoral counselling's obsession with the individual does not rest with counselling alone.*

The Absence of Genuine Community [7]

The problem of how to actualize the corporate reality of the church in contemporary life is far bigger than the problems

6. See also IV:20 and IV:22.
7. From E. E. Thornton, *Theology and Pastoral Counseling* (Philadelphia, Fortress Press, Prentice-Hall, 1964), pp.125–6.

inherent in the nature of pastoral counseling. Pastoral counseling in its privatized form is a symptom, not a cause, of the absence of genuine community in the institutionalized church. It is in one sense an interim form of ministry. Pastoral counseling symbolizes the potential concern of a church that has lost its power effectively to actualize its concern for troubled people. The absence of true *koinonia* in the church calls for more serious attention to the immediate task of equipping ministers for counseling as a representative ministry of the whole church. It calls for more imaginative developments within the counseling movement – such as . . . group counseling . . . Ultimately, it calls for the equipping of ministers not only as counselors but also as 'equippers' or training supervisors of the laity. The minister would become a true 'teaching elder' were he equipped for the equipping of the laity for pastoral ministry. Only when entire congregations accept corporate responsibility for shepherding, and only when laymen, as well as ministers, are adequately prepared for counseling ministries will it be possible to say that in reality 'the church *is* the counselor'.

VI:33

From the same stable as Lambourne and Mathers, but in the succeeding generation of teachers at Birmingham, Stephen Pattison shows a similar alertness in his writing to issues about the integrity of the disciplines of pastoral studies and practical theology. Pastoral studies, as he points out in an article elsewhere,[8] is not training in specific skills such as counselling or community work. Pastoral skills may result, but pastoral studies includes evaluation of these skills; and its main aim is 'to develop critical reflection on and knowledge of, environment, society, the person and theology in relation to the pastoral task'.[9] In this extract from a symposium on 'The Foundation of Pastoral Studies' Pattison critically evaluates the use of the behavioural sciences (including psychotherapy and counselling) in practical theology.

8. S. Pattison, 'Pastoral Studies: Dust Bin or Discipline' (*Contact* 80, 1983:3, pp. 22–6).
9. ibid., p. 23.

Some Limitations in the Use of Behavioural Sciences [10]

1. *Selection of human sciences*

. . . Within pastoral studies there are those using insights drawn from most of the mainstream human sciences but so far little attempt has been made critically to assess the relative significance and importance of particular disciplines. Each social science has implicit views of the nature of being human. The adequacy and coherence of different disciplines ought to be evaluated. It may be that some social sciences provide clearer, more comprehensive or more theologically compatible accounts of the human condition than do others. . . .

2. *Selection of aspects of the various human sciences*

In a recent book Malcolm Jeeves, an academic psychologist, outlines the diversity within contemporary psychology and warns against treating it as a monolithic entity. He indicates that the assertion 'psychology says' is likely to denote a superficial acquaintance with the discipline.[11] The wide variety of different approaches to be found in any one behavioural science is further underlined in Windy Dryden's account of individual therapies in Britain.[12] Dryden identifies at least 12 types of psychotherapy each of which has its own undergirding theoretical framework and often a philosophy to match. Similarly, the divide between Marxist and functionalist sociologists is in every way as real as that between psychodynamically-oriented psychologists who draw on the theories of Freud and behaviouristic psychologists who draw on those of Skinner. Pastoral studies must not only select particular disciplines but it must also discriminate between different aspects or schools within them.

3. *The problem of relevance*

A teacher or researcher trying to understand unemployment and its implications may turn to the literature of economics, politics, psychology, sociology, anthropology, geography or other disciplines. The problem is that their time, energy, knowledge and expertise are likely to be limited. The question then arises as to

10. From S. Pattison, 'The Use of the Behavioural Sciences in Practical Theology' in P. H. Ballard (ed.), *The Foundations of Pastoral Studies and Practical Theology* (University College Cardiff, The Board of Studies for Pastoral Studies, 1986), pp. 79–85.
11. M. A. Jeeves (ed.), *Behavioural Sciences: A Christian Perspective* (IVP, 1984).
12. W. Dryden (ed.), *Individual Therapy in Britain* (London, Harper and Row, 1984).

where attention should be focussed. In the case of unemployment, for instance, it may be that ultimately the most illuminating picture is presented by, say, macro-economic theory and that this is therefore the most relevant discipline. If the teacher has no knowledge of economics but is very interested and competent in the field of, say, counselling there is a strong possibility that the situation will be considered from the perspective of the psychological effects that unemployment may have on the individual. Here again it is probable that particular types of psychological theory, e.g. those concerning loss, may be preferred as being more 'relevant' than others. Such a preference may be influenced by a person's own strongly-held and rationally-supported convictions. It may also be influenced by less admirable factors like the availability and accessibility of the literature. It is important, therefore, for those involved in pastoral studies to be clear and overt about the limits of their own vision, competence and ideological preferences so that particular disciplines or aspects of disciplines are not exalted to a position of supreme relevance which they might not deserve. . . .

4. Eclecticism

Many of those working within pastoral studies boast a cheerfully eclectic approach. They draw insights, methods and skills from different sources, disciplines, and aspects of disciplines in order to attain understanding or effect change. Those whose reflection on eclecticism has gone no further than to acknowledge that they themselves adopt this approach might be sobered by Dryden's identification of no less than 10 species of this activity within the theory and practice of individual therapy. One in particular should perhaps command attention, which Dryden denotes 'haphazard eclecticism'. This is scathingly criticized because some therapists are likely to choose their theories, models and techniques on the basis of subjective appeal; 'I use whatever makes sense to me and whatever I feel comfortable with' is a frequent refrain. . . . There is only a thin line between a search for valid and truthful perspectives in many different disciplines and being a thoroughgoing dilettante who has no understanding of the assumptions and limitations of the discipline from which a particular insight might come and with which it may be ineffably tainted. . . . It is tempting and relatively easy to trawl through the human sciences and assemble a series of insights drawn from many disciplines which may then implicitly or explicitly be claimed to be of great significance and worth. . . .

141

5. *Going native*

For some the danger is not that they fail adequately to understand particular human sciences but that they become so entranced by them they abandon their objective, or perhaps their distinctively theological perspective. In other words, they 'go native'. This tendency has perhaps been most apparent in pastoral psychology and pastoral counselling, particularly in America. It is easy to find books and articles which seem to contain much psychology but little theological evaluation or insight. This is a criticism which could be leveled at some recent British contributions to the literature of pastoral care. Authors demonstrate a detailed expert knowledge of other subjects but any theology which might be there is really only implicit. Sadly, it would seem that some in the field are only at home in non-theological disciplines and have neither the desire nor perhaps the ability to offer any theological critique of those disciplines. There is some evidence[13] that this danger is being increasingly recognized. . . .

6. *Pastoral pragmatism*

Many within pastoral studies would not regard themselves as first and foremost scholars. In the main their studies in other disciplines are determined and called forth by the need to understand the world, or particular situations within it, so appropriate action can be taken to change or preserve it. They in some sense seek clear indications or 'answers'. There is, therefore, a constant temptation to look for neatly packaged epigrams for the sake of pastoral utility. . . . Qualifications and hesitancies in the face of a complex reality make poor rallying cries for dynamic pastoral action, but it is worth reflecting that while the truth is seldom simple it is something about which those in pastoral studies should have a concern. Complexity should not always be sacrificed to convenience.

7. *Anachronism*

This arises out of the contemporary explosion of knowledge. It is very difficult indeed to keep up to date and so there is a real danger of anachronism, i.e. relying on facts or opinions which have been superceded or found to be of doubtful value. Thinkers like Freud and Jung, for instance, continue to be of great interest to theologians while their influence has been of declining importance in psychology as a whole. At the same time other aspects of

13. The author gives Oden (see I:2) as an example.

psychology have been developed which have been almost
ignored. . . .

8. *Mediocrity*
The scope of the social sciences, the very partial knowledge of
teachers and researchers, rapid developments in many disciplines,
the variety of subjects which must be coped with leaves pastoral
studies open on many occasions to the charge of mediocrity. When
thinking in this area seems no more than a free association of
ideas drawn from dubious 'pop' psychology or dated paperback
sociology and words like 'God' or 'incarnation', it is tempting to
see the charge as justified. An interdisciplinary activity can be a
stimulus to enormous practical and intellectual vigour and rigour
in which different ways of seeing the world are brought alongside
one another. It can also be an excuse for laziness and the manufacture of vague generalities. One measure of excellence in interdisciplinary endeavour would be that it would begin to formulate its
own insights and interpretations which were of sufficient weight
to command some attention and respect in other relevant disciplines. It would, therefore, perhaps be desirable to see those
engaged in pastoral studies making worthwhile if modest contributions to disciplines like psychology, sociology, or social
work. . . .

VI:34

*One critique of pastoral counselling is its lack of relationship with
the Church and with theology; another is of its uncritical selection
from or absorption of other disciplines. We might add that even
when pastoral counselling tries to become theologically respectable,
it can also plunder theology uncritically for parallels to support its
own assumptions and values. There is a third, equally powerful
criticism, which at ground level often comes from those who work
on the political and/or community issues, that counselling tends
towards helping the oppressed to conform or to tolerate oppression,
and does not challenge or try to change the very structures that
oppress. I have addressed this in a limited way in my introduction,
which attempts to build a bridge across this apparent gulf. The
critique is equally to be found in some theologians: two readings,
one from either side of the Atlantic, illustrate the arguments.*

*Shirley Guthrie appears, on the surface, to be describing only
the current values in the Church as narcissistic. In fact what he calls
the 'old moralism or idealism' to which he does not wish the Church*

143

to return, is probably equally narcissistic, inasmuch as being seen to be altruistic can make people feel good about themselves, less guilty, etc. This leads one to wonder whether even the political spirituality he advocates as the 'truth' might not also disguise selfish motives. Perhaps in the end it is motivation, whether in self-sacrifice, self-affirmation, or Kingdom theology which determines the authenticity of any of these three ways of interpreting the will of God.

From Pious Narcissism to Political Spirituality [14]

Once upon a time, there was a bunch of very uptight people. They believed in being trustworthy, loyal, helpful, friendly, courteous, kind, obedient, thrifty, cheerful, brave, clean and reverent. They tried to put self out of the way to do their duty to God and their country, and to make their parents proud of them.

Along came some psychiatrists and ministers and pastoral counselors and theologians and told these good hard-working, God-fearing, mentally awake and morally straight people: You're sick. You need to quit doing someone else's thing and do your own thing. You don't have to put yourself down and try to be something you are not. You're OK. Be yourself. Hang loose. Be free. Get off your head trip and trust your feelings. Stop taking care of everyone else and start taking care of yourself. Get your own needs met and stop worrying so much about everyone else's needs.

And a lot of people listened to this advice. It was difficult for some of them to put into practice such self-affirmation after they had thought for so many years that self-denial was what they should strive for. But it wasn't impossible. After all, they lived in a society which had always thought highly of itself – a society which thought the rest of the world was there to provide the resources for its consumption and a market for its products; a society which was the most powerful and most virtuous country in the world, whose way of life all other countries either wanted to adopt or should be forced to adopt. And, after all, they were daily assured by TV that the whole purpose of life is to entertain, beautify, deodorize, tranquilize, satisfy and pleasurize oneself. And, after all, their religious leaders had told them that their own and their nation's salvation is the most important of all religious questions.

14. From S. C. Guthrie, 'The Narcissism of American Piety: The Disease and the Cure' (*The Journal of Pastoral Care*, vol. xxxi, no. 4, December 1977, pp. 220–9).

So a lot of people made it. Self-affirmation and doing your own thing was in and self-sacrifice and doing your duty was out. Thinking was out and feeling was in. Personal relationships and social commitments were legitimate and binding only so long as and to the extent that they contributed to self-actualization and happiness.

Then the psychiatrists, preachers, pastoral counselors and theologians began to say: That's not exactly what we had in mind. In fact, that's sick. It's sick to think you are the center of the universe. You are living like spoiled children instead of like mature adults. You can't just act on the basis of your feelings of the moment; you have to consider the consequences of your actions. Where are your moral values? Your sense of responsibility? Your self-discipline? Your sensitivity to the needs and feelings of other people? Your awareness of human community? And they began to write articles and discuss among themselves how they could help cure the blatant narcissism some of them acknowledged they themselves were partly responsible for.

That is the issue I want to address. . . .

So what I want to do is (1) ask how we religious people have supported or at least allowed the narcissism of our time: (2) ask how we can correct it without returning to the old moralism or idealism we have quite properly left behind us. Specifically, I want to suggest three interrelated lines of thought which seem to me to be promising ways of dealing with the open or hidden pious narcissism of our time.

1. The Truth about God

In the first place, if we are to overcome and find a legitimate alternative to the narcissism of American piety, we have to discover for ourselves and then tell the truth about God.

One psychiatrist has defined the narcissist as a person for whom others are like a candy machine. We have taught people, or at least allowed them to believe, that God is the great heavenly candy machine. The candy he dispenses varies according to different theological emphases. In my introduction, I dealt primarily with existentialists (whether they call themselves that or not) for whom the candy is self-fulfilment. But in principle there is no difference between them and fundamentalists for whom it is personal salvation. Or charismatics for whom it is personal joy, peace and religious ecstasy. Or liberals for whom it is the victory of whatever cause or movement they identify themselves with. . . .

We might as well tell the truth, because more and more people are catching on anyway. The candy machine is busted. . . . The truth is that God is not the great heavenly dispenser of spiritual, material and psychological goodies. He is the weak, vulnerable, suffering God who can be recognized only in a despised Jew hanging from Nazi gallows in the twentieth century, the same God who was identified with another despised Jew hanging on a cross in the first century. The God who is always to be found, not in victory over, but identified with human weakness and guilt and suffering and death. . . .

So the truth is not that 'God will take care of you' but that God *cares* for you – cares enough to involve himself in the world he loves, to risk being hurt by it, to share the pain it both causes and suffers, even to die for it. And if he is that kind of God, then believing in him and serving him does not result in being taken care of; it means caring as he cares, risking oneself as he risks himself and accepting the consequences of such caring and risking. 'Finding God' does not solve our problems and get us out of trouble; it gives us more difficult problems and gets us into even more trouble. It makes life not easier but harder. . . .

Loving (*doing* not just *feeling* love) *is* real self-fulfillment and salvation and getting one's needs met. . . . If such loving is costly and painful, it is not because God and those who love like him believe that suffering in itself is good (as masochists believe) but because they believe that *loving* is good, no matter what the cost. The fulfillment of God's deity and our humanity depend on it.

And when pious narcissists learn that, then there will be no need for a religion and ethic based on bribes to get people to do what they ought to, or threats to scare them into it. There will be no need for any moralistic talk about responsibility, duty, commitment and consideration of others. All that will take care of itself. . . .

2. The Truth about Ourselves
If we are going to overcome and find a legitimate alternative to the narcissism of American piety, we have not only to stop telling lies and start telling the truth about God (which is also the truth about ourselves): we have to stop telling lies and start telling the truth about ourselves (which is also the truth about God).

The worst lie we have told people is that they are OK, that God accepts them just as they are and that they can therefore accept themselves just as they are. Our intentions were good, of course. We were combating a perverted religion that taught people that it is bad to be human and that they ought to despise themselves. . . .

How then can we help set people free from the pious romantic narcissism which will always finally be exposed as the godless,

146

inhuman narcissism it really was under the surface from the very beginning? The answer is not to take back or qualify the good news of God's free grace, but to come to a better understanding of what that grace means. Nor is the answer to begin telling people again how *unacceptable* they are; we have to talk not about what they *are* at all, good *or* bad, but about what they can *become*. Nor, once again, is the answer to begin preaching about personal commitment, social responsibility, self-denial, moral values and the like; we have to begin living and proclaiming *hope* – hope in God and therefore hope for ourselves, for other people and for the world we live in. Hope, of course, has come to mean Moltmann[15], and it is in fact he who I think has most clearly seen what needs to be said also in this context. . . .

Now that kind of grace puts a clear end to all narcissistic *or* masochistic acceptance of self, others or world as they are. It makes people *dissatisfied* and *unwilling* to defend and justify what they themselves are or what other people are. It makes people *maladjusted* in the society in which they live, perpetually *unhappy* with the state of the world around them. But at the same time it will not allow them to settle for the pessimistic attitude that nothing can ever change, except for the worse. Grace that is both accepting *and* transforming grace 'infects people with hope' (Moltmann) – hope for themselves *and* for other people *and* for the world. And where there is hope, there is confidence not only in the possibility but in the necessity of *change*, impatient eagerness not to *be* but to *become*, courage to get on with the business of moving into a new and different future. . . .

Such a *narcissism-ending confidence in the future* is obviously not easy either to achieve in ourselves or to instill in others. But is it any more difficult than a romantic *narcissism-producing faith in the present* which tries to convince ourselves and others that God accepts us just as we are, that we can therefore accept ourselves just as we are, and that everything is beautiful? The real question, however, is not whether pious people *can* believe the promises of God's transforming grace and the hope and change it brings, but whether they really *want* to. This question leads me to the final point I want to make.

3. The Truth about Spirituality
If we are to overcome and find a legitimate alternative to the narcissism of American piety, we have to expose all the various

15. J. Moltmann, *The Crucified God* (London, SCM Press, 1976), *The Power of the Powerless* (London, SCM Press, 1983).

forms of fake spirituality which are popular in our time. We can do that only when we know what true spirituality is and become truly spiritual people ourselves.

Many observers have noted that in our technological, bureaucratic, impersonal and depersonalizing society, people are hungry for a spiritual dimension in life that will give them a sense of meaning and excitement and aliveness in the midst of all the boredom, deadness and emptiness around them. Some turn to various forms of real or pseudo Eastern religion, with or without a little Western existentialism and/or back-to-nature romanticism thrown in. Others seek charismatic ecstasy. Others seek a church or church-substitute where they can participate in what one critic has called 'hand-holding, heart-baring, soul-sharing, happiness-oriented, relational, interpersonal piety'. . . .

But we can be truly compassionate with those who are searching for the Spirit in all the directions I have mentioned when we let them know that they are looking for him where he is not to be found. Whether they search the depths of their own inner selves, or the breadth of the universe, or the intimate fellowship of other persons; whether they try to rise *above* or explore the depths *below* or plunge *into* or look to the *end* of everyday human experience; whether their search is openly religious or supposedly only psychological; whether or not they call themselves Christians – none of them will find what they are looking for unless they first discover the Spirit in the *one* place where he is really 'at home'. Unless he is found there, he will not be recognized anywhere. Unless he is encountered there, people will never know the 'fellowship of the Holy Spirit' but only the lonely isolation of their own starved spirits. . . . Where is the place of the Spirit? The Bible says (to quote a well-known preacher) that it is where *justice* is being done. Not first of all where people have private mystical or charismatic experiences. Not where people 'share' with each other and have 'meaningful' personal relationships in small group meetings in a psychiatrist's office or in a church or in a home prayer circle. Not in Eastern *or* Western religion. Where *justice* is done. Not blind neutral justice but *real* justice. Justice which is openly and actively biased in favor of those who are poor and hungry, ignored and forgotten, excluded, exploited and oppressed. . . . True spirituality, in other words, is not found either in the religious *or* in the psychological sphere but in the economic and political sphere which deals with such apparently 'unspiritual' things as hunger, human rights, US economic policies abroad, social welfare, racism in housing patterns and public

148

education, and the way in which energy resources are managed. . . .

Two things follow from this political spirituality:

1. . . . to the extent that we have talked about the *Spirit* of God apart from the *Kingdom* of God in the world we have sponsored a false spirituality, a spirituality which may talk piously of God, love, hope and Holy Spirit but is really nothing but pious narcissism without God, without other people, and therefore without a really human self.

2. But the second thing is also true: If we preachers and counselors and theologians do hear what the Bible says about who the Holy Spirit is, and if we really trust people when they say they are hungry for the spiritual dimension in life, then there will be no need to continue the old debate about individual freedom versus social responsibility. Or about whether individuals are there for the sake of society or society for the sake of individuals. Or whether we should change individuals in order to change society or change society in order to change individuals. Or whether personal evangelism or social action is more important. Those will all be exposed as the false alternatives they are, and the one right issue will emerge. For the sake of both individuals *and* 'society', both personal salvation *and* social solidarity, in this world *and* the next: What does the justice of the Kingdom of God which the Holy Spirit brings look like? Which economic and political policies, movements, strategies and goals point most clearly in that direction? What action can Spirit-filled people take to move in that direction?

VI:35

Professor Dyson of Manchester University examines a different issue, the development of pastoral theology; he too challenges individualism, but adds to the argument the type of 'one-way' pastoral relationship which, on appearances at least, is typical of much pastoral counselling. He reminds us of the critique which socialism and feminism make, of individualism and hierarchical distancing respectively. In this article Dyson is actually describing pastoral theology as a whole, of which pastoral counselling is but one part; but as part, it must share in the total analysis.

A Critique of Pastoral Practice and Pastoral Theology [16]

The origins and modern development of pastoral theology must now seriously be called into question for a number of reasons. Some of these also relate to theology in general and I mention these first before noting others which have a special reference to pastoral theology.

First, pastoral theology has to involve itself in the wider debate about the authority of the Bible and tradition, and of the meaning and content which may be given to the notion of revelation in relation to other sources of knowledge to which pastoral theology refers.

Second, pastoral theology is involved with the question of the historical Jesus and of the extent to which He may be regarded as the historical and/or theological norm for pastoral theology and practice.

Third, pastoral theology has to take note of the related issues concerning the time-bound character of theological statements. How far are the various traditional themes and outlooks of pastoral theology determined by prevailing cultures and what interpretative procedures are available to work with these questions?

I now turn to a series of challenges which bear upon pastoral theology more particularly.

First, pastoral theology will be required to register, as theological ethics has to some extent already done, a greater interest in the debates in the sciences about the nature and determinants of the self. The warm personalism of much pastoral theology, still thinking of an independent self-directing consciousness largely unaffected by physical and social processes, must give way to more complex and more severe accounts of the self.

Second, the challenge to individualism, which in political economy has come from various forms of socialism, and which in social work has come from community work, must now make itself felt against individualistic pastoral theology, perhaps from the direction of political and liberation theology. What is at stake are not only questions of the correct human locus for pastoral theology, but also the further challenge as to whether pastoral theology's traditional concern with the individual does not fall prey to the charge of manipulation, of a social control which actually *inhibits* social change and individual development.

16. From A. O. Dyson, 'Pastoral Theology: Towards a New Discipline' (*Contact*, 78, 1983:1, pp. 2–8).

Third, the practice-based origins of pastoral theology have already been in part challenged by the increasing professionalization of the clergy (parallel with professionalization in other spheres too), where a body of theory and practice is evolved which is more sophisticated in content but which serves to keep a closed profession closed. Also, paradoxically, this very process of professionalization has become confused because the nature and function of the clergy is no longer clear to clergy or to their clients. Connected with that lack of clarity is a rising *lay*-self-consciousness which blurs the image of the clergy and fundamentally questions the notion that pastoral theology is the preserve of clergy.

Fourth, it is a commonplace, though an important one, that the rapid extension of pastoral-social work by statutory and voluntary agencies since the nineteenth century raises searching questions about whose practice pastoral theology refers to, and *to whom* that practice is directed.

Fifth, practice-based pastoral theology is seen by some as theologically imbued with a 'Pelagian' optimism about humankind. So in one form or another (e.g. Barthianism) a plea arises for the restoration of a more transcendental, supernaturalist, judgemental quality of this discipline. This and other similar pleas clearly pose a searching question to pastoral theology about its necessary connections with a particular announcement of good news (gospel) in all its radical challenge.

Sixth, feminist theology has, in my opinion, succeeded in demonstrating beyond reasonable doubt the largely androcentric character of Christian tradition in theology and church practice. The resultant attempts to reconstruct the doctrine of the human person in the light of that criticism have direct consequences for pastoral theology. For example, the possibility that the character of the religious quest may be quite different in men and women must put a question-mark upon a range of pastoral beliefs, assumptions, practices, rituals shaped by the androcentric tradition. Again, if it is correct that notions of hierarchy, of distancing the 'other', are products of the androcentric tradition, pastoral theology may have to revise some of its most basic assumptions about the nature and purpose of interventions into people's lives.

Seventh, and last, I want to draw especial attention to a challenge which seems in some respects recent and relatively unexamined. The inherited practice-based theology used, consciously or unconsciously, the concept of *apprenticeship*. For the most part, ministers would work out their pastoral theology in the early years of their ministry largely through imitation of older and allegedly wiser ministers. Thus the *theoretical* basis of pastoral practice was not seriously addressed. Doubts and difficulties would be resolved within the terms of the apprentice-relationship. The study, on any serious scale, of theoretical subjects in the pastoral sphere as a precondition of ordination was certainly not required in the Church of England. This state of affairs has changed only recently with the result that *pastoral studies* has rapidly grown in importance and curricular visibility in many theological colleges and seminaries. In this rise to prominence of pastoral studies, confusion and conflict understandably reign in many quarters. . . . The problems which arise today in pastoral studies reflect similar problems in education and social work: the question of theory; supervised practice; the pattern of interdisciplinarity. But these problems are compounded by the deep emotions variously felt as people bemoan or rejoice at the loss of simplicity, at the tendencies to politicisation, all overlaid by the obsessive anachronisms of British divisions of churchmanship. . . .

I turn now to consider briefly why a disciplined response to these challenges is more than a domestic churchly matter.

1. It seems clear that Christian (systematic) theology will not long sustain itself as a credible discipline with bearing upon social realities as long as it retains the generalized and abstract character it has traditionally possessed. This is not to deny that there is a continuing place for systematic, philosophical and doctrinal theology. But the complexity, fluctuation and multi-sided change of societies in late, middle or early stages of modernization point to the need for *mediating, flexible, applied disciplines* which can relate adequately to these modern conditions without being engulfed by them. Pastoral theology appears to be the theological discipline potentially most easily developable in these terms.

2. After decades of relative buoyancy and self-confidence, perhaps deriving from the traditions of Victorian middle-class philanthropy, many of the caring professions, and the bodies of theory attached to them, are in disarray. On a widespread scale, rational enquiry about ends and means is being replaced by strident appeals to ideology, by a new conservatism which simply reintroduces all the unresolved problems of practice-based work, or by a pragmatism in which moral ideals and values disappear from the vocabulary, and where preoccupation with theory is regarded as pretentious and irrelevant. If, as for example in penal theory and practice, the most fundamental purposes are now in question,

is it possible to envisage pastoral theology finding a secular voice and discovering a public vocation?

3. In the Christian sphere there is a good deal of evidence today of sinister gaps between believing and praying, and between praying and exercising worldly responsibility. For complex historical reasons theology, ethics, spirituality have lost their connections with each other, and each with a secularizing society. Again the only discipline potentially in contact simultaneously with all three areas might appear to be pastoral theology, which, in this case, would increasingly have to be accorded a greater primacy among the theological disciplines, indeed as a discipline to which the others significantly contribute.

I have deliberately cast these three remarks about the potential wider utility of pastoral theology in broad terms. I accept that this kind of reasoning would have to be expounded in much greater detail. But the limited remarks made are intended to serve at least as an indication that in my view the question of pastoral theology is both more important and more comprehensive than is often allowed. . . .

Public Vocation

It is surely justified, as some writers have done, to raise questions about expressions of pastoral theology which simply take over the norms of other disciplines with the addition of a thin theological veneer. For pastoral theology is part of theology, a discipline which makes a series of striking claims about the world – claims which are not easily accommodated without loss to the positions of other sciences. This is an important question, not only at the intellectual level, but at the level of pastoral practice too. Is pastoral theology obliged to fit in with the assumptions and conventions of the wider intellectual firmament? Is pastoral practice in a Christian context part of a roughly homogeneous group of helping-caring activities in society? Has pastoral theology a distinctive Christian axis?

Some of these questions are helpfully, if indirectly, explored in a recent essay by Donald Houston on 'Affirmation and Sacrifice in Everyday Life and in Social Work'.[17] Houston distinguishes between *unilateral* affirmation where each person is who he or she is without much regard to the experience and enactment of the being of others. *Reciprocal* affirmation is where each person

17. In N. Timms and D. Watson (eds.), *Philosophy of Social Work* (London, Routledge and Kegan Paul, 1978), pp. 180–204.

experiences himself or herself in the light of an awareness of how other persons are experiencing themselves. Houston argues that most relationships in contemporary British society are of the unilateral type where we always define ourselves as winners in relation to others as losers. . . .

Houston's is an important argument which can be developed from another direction in terms of feminist theology's treatment of the theme of *hierarchy*. Houston's account must by implication be very critical of various kinds of one-way pastoral relationships in which the identity and position of the carer is not called into question. Such an indictment would, for example, probably be true of almost all of the churches' pastoral responses to the 'working classes' since the beginning of the industrial revolution. It would also be true of many types of formal counselling in which clergy are engaged. But these unilateral assumptions flourishing in Christian context are incompatible with basic Christian assertions about the mutual self-giving of God and human persons, in a reciprocity of grace and freedom, and about the self-giving to others of the Incarnation. It would seem to me that pastoral theology should expect to explore the reciprocal mode in all its aspects of nothing less than an exposition of the Gospel. . . .

I have tried here to show how it is possible to begin critically relating pastoral theology on the one hand to fundamental theology, and, on the other hand, to social and political arrangements about us. It is possible to see how, without ceasing to learn from other disciplines, without retiring from the fray, it is quite possible, on a Christian argumentation, to come up with a direction of social policy which is radically untypical of current practice, but which cannot be ignored simply because it differs from the prevailing wisdom. This can however only be done if we are also prepared to probe critically a Christian tradition redolent of androcentrism, hierarchy and the unilateral mode.

VI:36

Dr Peter Selby, Bishop of Kingston, wrote the paper from which the final extract is taken, when he was working as a diocesan missioner in north-east England, before the eighties' idolatry of monetarism. He was at that time particularly concerned with priorities in mission, bringing to his task pastoral care and counselling training and experience. He found that caring for individuals always raises ultimate questions about the nature of society, and

154

has explored this more fully in 'Liberating God'.[18] *In this paper he likewise helps bridge the apparent divide between pastoral care of the individual and the prophetic mission to society, through the parallel between the unconscious forces in the individual and also in society.*

'We cannot unlearn . . .' [19]

The Christian proclamation is concerned fundamentally with the end of the reign of the idols. The Christian task has therefore to do with the smashing of the idols as the sign of the end of their reign. In a post-Christian, post-religious era this fundamental proclamation and this basic task may seem to have lost their relevance. If gods of all kinds are on the wane and religious observance of any kind on the decrease, the basic orientation of Christians against idolatry may seem to be less important than it used to be.

Yet to take this attitude is to allow an unnecessary literalism to obscure the spirit of the task. The absence of labels on certain objects declaring them to be idols is no more a guarantee that idols no longer exist than the rise of secularism is a guarantee that 'worship' is no longer a strong – and perhaps highly dangerous? – feature of the lives of people. To suggest that one way of looking at the rise in the pastoral care movement is that it is part of the end of the reign of the idols is to give it a theological context which may serve to illuminate some of the challenges which face us in the future.

Idols basically have to do with man's sense of his own contingency and they witness to a failure of confidence in his own worth and ultimate survival. The worship of idols proclaims, explicitly usually, and implicitly always, the notion that human worth and even human survival are conditional upon surrender to, and frequently appeasement of, certain basic forces in nature and in the nature of things, that manage at the same time to be both immutable and unreliable. They are immutable because they are not under human control, and they are unreliable because their forces cannot be predicted and their consequences for human life cannot be judged in advance. Human life has therefore to be lived on the edge of both terror and worthlessness. The ritual and

18. P. Selby, *Liberating God: Private Care and Public Struggle* (London, SPCK, 1983).
19. From an unpublished paper by P. Selby, 'The One and the Many – the Transcendent in Pastoral Care'.

magic that are developed for the purpose of taming these basically immutable and unreliable forces derive power not from the fact that in any scientific sense can they be judged to work, but from the fact that since the forces concerned are both immutable and unreliable there is nothing else to be done. That happens (and it is no mere coincidence) to be politically highly convenient for those in positions of power. The doctrine that life is lived in the midst of immutability and unreliability provides a buttress for the arbitrary exercise of power and a perpetual alibi for that arbitrariness.

The proclamation of the end of the reign of the idols is thus a proclamation of the end of the rule of immutability and unreliability in human affairs. It is the proclamation that human survival and human worth do not in the last resort depend on surrender to, or appeasement of, forces outside human control, but upon the disciplining of those forces which are within human control, in accordance with values which are themselves consistent with human worth and responsibility. The doctrine, spelt out at the end of the creation myth, that man is in charge of the natural order, is not there to encourage man to take up a position in relation to nature akin to that of a tyrant in relation to society. Rather it elevates human responsibility and worth over against forces which hold man in a net that is both immutable and unreliable, and which therefore make life fundamentally free of values. The end of the reign of the idols means that life can never be free of values because it is not out of control.

The rise of the human sciences and the growth of psychotherapeutic skills have ironically been proclaimed as the latest form of determinism to enslave us. The reverse is true. The more we know of the development of the human mind and the great forces at work in the human unconscious, the less we need to approach them with superstition. The more we understand the development of human sexuality or of the way in which the need for survival bears fruit in either expressed or repressed aggression, the less immutable and unreliable these great human drives become. While they were unknown and the objects of terror they could not be subject to direction and control by human beings in accordance with their highest values. Having examined them scientifically and clinically we know that we are on the road to a place where basic human drives do not confront us with the demand for surrender or appeasement. On the contrary, they offer opportunities for human freedom and responsibility. . . .

It is painfully obvious that the idols do not surrender so quickly, or so easily. Such statements about the end of terror and superstition in relation to the workings of the human unconscious may appear quite hopelessly bland when considered alongside the difficulties and uncertainties of research, and the pain and struggle involved in the quest for personal growth. There is plenty of life in the idols yet.

That is all true. Yet the reign of an idol is at an end, not just when every last sign of its resistance has disappeared, but when human beings make the decision, in any sphere of life, to move away from superstition and towards control. In the way of that movement are numerous obstacles. Yet the decision once taken is irrevocable, and in that sense once the decision has been taken to move away from idolatry, the reign of the idols is at an end. . . .

The most worrying features of where we now find ourselves are the signs of reaction and of a determination, if it were possible, to rehabilitate old superstitions and taboos. Under the guise of the desire to move back to 'moral standards' there is appearing a strident preference for ignorance and a desire to turn our backs on all the most precious things that we have discovered about how persons can develop creatively. . . . We need to be very clear that signs of reaction, even violent reaction, and even reaction that looks like being quite successful for a time, do not negate fundamental human decisions to end the reign of the idols. In relation to personal development that decision has clearly been made. We cannot unlearn what we have so painfully learned. . . .

One of the fascinating features of the development of the pastoral care movement has been the growing awareness that it is precisely the concern for the life and growth of the individual which has been the lifeblood of the movement, that carries with it the danger that a whole host of other influences on the lives of persons will go unexamined and uncriticised. Thus they will be left as immutable and unreliable forces dominant in human living. Hardly any conference of practitioners of pastoral care takes place without there coming from some corner of the room the demand that the political and social dimensions of the problem being examined should be adequately considered. It is precisely those who are most involved and become most closely aware of the intricacies of people's lives who should at the same time be clearest about the enormity of the forces and pressures which threaten to overwhelm us. The concern with the development of individuals, and assisting them to struggle with their deepest feelings, must not be allowed to turn into a cult of intimacy in which the small and private become the last remaining areas of meaning in a world implicitly proclaimed to be governed by immutable and unreliable forces.

The forces that govern the world are immutable and unreliable, and are therefore idols, only if we choose to make them so. The fact that the control and even the understanding of the big battalions of economic power is difficult does not mean that it is to be left unattempted; the fact that there are vast numbers of votes to be gained in policies based upon quite straightforward and ever more frequently declared racialism does not mean that we cease to struggle to find a way in which a world of vastly rich and varied cultures can discover a way towards a just peace.

Here it is important to understand that idolatry does not consist in private sins or even the aggregate of private sins. People are not worshipping money, that is to say treating money as an idol, when they simply want more of it; and they are not doing homage to the idol of race simply when they dislike a person of a different colour. Idolatry consists in ascribing supernatural meaning to natural objects, and magical power to things which are essentially subject to human control. The worship of money is expressed in the view that social progress is *dependent* on greater wealth rather than the other way round. Personal greed for money is simply the individual expression of a totally accepted corporate assumption that without greater and greater wealth we cannot achieve more and more justice. That is to make human history subject not to human control but to a force which, though invented by human beings, has been given quasi-supernatural status. . . .

As we examine the history of the discipline or range of disciplines subsumed under the title 'pastoral care and counselling' the prophetic role of pastoral work becomes very clear, despite the fact that prophecy and pastoral care are most often seen as quite separate activities. Those who take upon themselves the care of persons are constantly confronted with situations to which pastoral care is no solution. No activity is more likely to expose the inadequacies of the idols of individualism than a profound concern with individuals. There is no surer way to dethrone the idol of intimacy, that is to say the viewing of intimacy as the only retreat from a harsh world, than the painful business of engaging with the intimate areas of one's own and other people's lives. Pastoral care has the capacity to give access to the transcendent, it points those who give and those who receive it beyond the problems which can be tackled by a pastor towards the whole range of issues that have to be faced in the quest for an inclusive and just, responsible and loving human fulfilment in the kingdom of God.

The processes involved in ending the reign of the idols are not such as can be completed in one activity or be summed up in one doctrine. They involve a constant, though self-critical, forward movement in which the insights derived from one activity, in this case pastoral care, stimulate new human adventures and challenge unexamined assumptions. The activity of pastoral care has shed a bright light on what human potential there is for love and acceptance and what value is to be placed on the honest facing of personal and corporate pain. That potential and that value cannot be realised in the activity of pastoral care alone, but those who have come to know this have much to say about those political and social assumptions which make their realisation so intensely difficult and so unequally distributed. In bearing witness to the insights which have emerged from their work, those involved in the practice and development of pastoral care are witnessing to the transcendence they have encountered. They are assisting our society to dethrone idols and so discover the immutable, though not in the least unreliable, fact that there is no god but God.

Index

Luther, M. 52–4, 68–9, 102, 105

magic 41, 98, 155–6, 158
marriage 14, 17, 119–23, 124
Marxism 140
Maslow, A. 46, 54, 88, 95, 114
Mass, Eucharist 27, 30 (*see also* Communion, Lord's Supper)
Mathers, J. 136–8, 139
maturity 58–9, 130
meaning *see* ultimate meaning
mental illness 81
ministry 16–18, 78–9, 80–4
Moltmann, J. 113, 147
monotheism 27–8, 48
moral thinking, morality 17, 37, 71, 107, 120–3, 157
moralism 143
mysticism 70; Eastern 53
myth 99, 115–18

narcissism 4, 16–18, 28, 34, 37, 59, 63, 65, 95, 130–6, 143–9
needs, spiritual 95
neurosis 22–5, 26–7, 30, 32, 35, 40, 53, 57, 77, 78–9, 94, 96
Niebuhr, R. 104
Nouwen, H. 87

Oden, T. 14–21
Odysseus 47
Oedipal feelings 27–8, 30
Oedipus 47
omnipotence 8, 49–50, 94
oppression 6

parental figures 22, 33
pastoral care: classical 15; definition of 9–10, 80
pastoral conversation 80, 84–7, 92–3

pastoral counselling: definition of 80, 124; movement 3
pastoral ministry 77–100
pastoral studies 7–8, 139–54
pastoral theology/theologians 7–8, 9, 12–13, 14–21, 65, 80, 87, 139–54
pathology, spiritual 98–100
Pattison, S. 139–43
Paul, St 28, 82, 102
peak-experiences 54–5, 95, 98
Pelagius 59, 151
penance 25
Perls, F. 15
Pfister, O. 25–6
phantasy 5, 6, 43, 119–23
Piaget, J. 101, 104, 111
piety 26
political theology and ministry 4–6, 144–9, 150–4, 155–9
politics 31, 140
polytheism 27–8
power 40, 61–5, 158
prayer 85, 107, 132
preaching 79, 85
primal father 29–32; murder 29–32
problems, religious 79, 95–100
professionalism 20–1, 36
professionalization 151–4
projection 50–1, 106, 122–3
prophetic ministry 4, 158–9
prophets 26
Protestantism, Protestant Church 20, 39–40, 86, 102
psyche *see* soul
psycho-history 52
psychoanalysis 25–6, 41, 61, 64, 65–6, 69
punishment 24

recapitulation 27–8
reconciliation 99
reconciling ministry 9–14, 82

redemption, definition of 126
Reformation, the 28, 102
religion: authentic 2–3, 32,
    94–5, 101, 144;
    authoritarian 2, 49–51, 60;
    definition of 3, 46, 49;
    healthy 2–3, 38;
    humanitarian 2–3, 49–51;
    inauthentic 2–3, 101;
    positive effects of 2–3, 38, 40
Renaissance, the 26, 28–9
reparation 31
representative persons 10, 21
repression 24, 26–9
resurrection 8, 37, 44, 90
revolution 35, 37
rituals 107, 155–6; meaningful
    99; obsessional 1, 22–5, 30;
    religious 1, 22–5, 30, 31, 36
Robinson, J. 66, 67, 69
Rogers, C. 15, 46, 56, 129
Roheim, G. 64
role of the pastor 77–100

sadism 65
salvation history 111
Scharfenberg, J. 80
Scheler, M. 61, 63
Schimmell, S. 71
Schultz, D. 16
security, search for 33
Selby, P. 154–9
self-actualization 54, 71, 145
self-consciousness 65
sentiment 57–8
sexuality 1, 24, 30, 36, 44, 75,
    87, 99, 107, 119–23, 156
shame 65
shepherding 19, 21, 87, 91, 139
sin 1, 8, 24, 34, 36, 51, 72, 82,
    83, 107, 110, 112, 126–7,
    158; definition of 124–5
Skinner, B. 15, 140
social work 153–4

society 4–6
sociology 140–3; of knowledge
    60
Socrates 50
Solignac, P. 35–7
soul, psyche 8, 41–4, 59
Spinoza, B. 50
Spirit, Holy 86, 98, 100, 111,
    148–9
spirit, living 42
spiritual direction/guidance 4,
    18, 73
spirituality, 93–100, 144–9
stages of faith, Fowler's 106,
    111
suffering 18, 41
Sullivan, H. 15, 111
superego 28, 30–1, 34, 37
supervision 12
Suzuki, D. 46
symbols, symbolism 22–3, 62,
    99, 115–18, 132

taboos 36–7, 107, 157
theology: see pastoral
    theology; crisis in 6–7,
    66–70; in pastoral
    counselling 124
Thornton, E. 80–4, 86–7, 92,
    138–9
Thurneysen, E. 80, 82, 84–7,
    92
Tillich, P. 46, 54, 55, 66, 69,
    82, 94, 104, 114–18
transcendence 98, 106, 128,
    158–9
transference 121
transpersonal essence 96
trust 105, 106

ultimate meaning, concern 10,
    41, 61–5, 94, 97, 101, 103,
    107, 115
unconditional acceptance 134